THE 5 MISTAKES EVERY INVESTOR MAKES AND HOW TO AVOID THEM

THE 5 MISTAKES

EVERY INVESTOR MAKES

AND HOW TO

AVOID THEM

Getting Investing **Right**

PETER MALLOUK

WILEY

Cover Design: Wiley
Cover Photograph: Crumpled Paper © iStock.com/borisyankov

Copyright © 2014 by John Wiley & Sons, Inc. All rights reserved.

Published by John Wiley & Sons, Inc., Hoboken, New Jersey.
Published simultaneously in Canada.

For general information on our other products and services or for technical support, please contact our Customer Care Department within the United States at (800) 762-2974, outside the United States at (317) 572-3993 or fax (317) 572-4002.

Wiley publishes in a variety of print and electronic formats and by print-on-demand. Some material included with standard print versions of this book may not be included in e-books or in print-on-demand. If this book refers to media such as a CD or DVD that is not included in the version you purchased, you may download this material at http://booksupport.wiley.com. For more information about Wiley products, visit www.wiley.com.

Library of Congress Cataloging-in-Publication Data:

Mallouk, Peter, 1970-
  The 5 mistakes every investor makes and how to avoid them:
getting investing right/Peter Mallouk.
      pages cm
  Includes bibliographical references and index.
  ISBN 978-1-118-92900-1 (hardback); ISBN 978-1-118-92902-5 (ePDF);
  ISBN 978-1-118-92901-8 (ePub)
  1. Investments. 2. Investment analysis. I. Title.
  HG4521.M285 2014
  332.6—dc23

                                        2014016780

Printed in the United States of America.

10 9 8 7 6 5 4 3

Contents

Preface

Over my career as a wealth manager, I have met thousands of individuals in search of a better way of investing. I noticed early on that most of the clients coming on board with my firm were terminating a prior advisor. It became clear to me that these clients weren't getting what they had hoped from their former advisors. While at times the issues were related to communication, relationships, and the like, sometimes the change was because the client wasn't getting the returns they had hoped or their former advisor had blown up their portfolio. Mistakes had been made along the way.

Many investors don't enjoy investing, don't have the time for it, or don't feel they are particularly good at it. It is this type of investor who searches for an advisor to alleviate the burden—to show them the way. Unfortunately, many if not most advisors make the same mistakes individuals often make. This is the tragedy of the financial services industry.

As I have watched fortunes made, lost, and sometimes rebuilt again, I have observed the main problems that led to the deterioration of wealth. The conclusion is quite simple: *In most cases, if an investor has greatly underperformed from an investment perspective, it is not because of the markets, but because of their own, or their advisor's own, mistakes.* All of us, at times, are susceptible to at least one of these mistakes. Many of the greatest investors of all time acknowledge they have made them, or are aware of them and actively put up mental roadblocks to prevent themselves from making them. For years, I have spoken about these mistakes, and this book will cover how to avoid these pitfalls as well as show a clear path toward achieving investment success.

Acknowledgments

This book wouldn't be possible without the ongoing efforts of Molly Rothove, Jessica Culpepper, James DeWitt, Brenna Stewart, and Jim Williams, all of whom contributed to this effort as well as to my newsletters, which are the constant source of in-house comedy prior to the editing process.

Special thanks to all of the incredibly talented people at Creative Planning, including those who helped with the research for the behavioral section of this book: Sarah Ayler, Kevin Dorsey, Andrew Horsman, Jeff Juday, Ashley Moulis, Meghan Perry, Conner Sivewright, Stacy Smith, and Chris Wolff.

A huge thank you to the clients of Creative Planning. I have learned so much from my clients over the years. Most importantly though, I learned that these are the type of people who make America what it is: the greatest place on earth to live. These folks make the economy go and grow and many of them have lived or are living the American Dream. My constant search for every possible way to help them has resulted in many of the things we do at my firm, and in the contents of this book.

To my mom who tricked me into believing I could do anything. I believed it until I was too old for it to matter. And to my dad, who taught me enough about investing at an early age that it became my passion. I especially cherish his advice to "ignore almost everything." Thanks to my beautiful wife Veronica, who spent a lot of time driving on our family road trips while I worked on this book, and to my three wonderful kids

Michael,* JP,† and Gabby‡ for always keeping me focused on the most important things in life.

Finally, thank you to those who helped edit and shape this book. All errors are my own.

* He must have asked half a dozen times: "Is anyone going to read this book?"
† Thanks for updating me on the NCAA tournament scores while I was writing.
‡ Thanks for the hugs, delivered almost every hour on the hour!

About the Author

Peter Mallouk is the #1 independent financial advisor in America (*Barron's*, August 2013). He is the President and Chief Investment Officer of Creative Planning, an independent advisory firm managing over $10 billion for clients in all 50 states.

Peter has made appearances on CNBC, CNBC Worldwide, and Fox Business News, and has been interviewed by the *Wall Street Journal*, CNBC.com, Yahoo! Finance, and many other financial news providers. He graduated from the University of Kansas in 1993 with four majors, including business administration and economics, and went on to earn a law degree and master of business administration in 1996, also at the University of Kansas. He has also earned the Certified Financial Planner designation.

Peter lives in Kansas City with his wife, Veronica, and their three children.

The Market Wants to Be Your Friend

Risk comes from not knowing what you are doing.

—Warren Buffett

Y ou might be wondering why this book appears to be flipping you the bird right out of the box (see Figure I.1).[1] Well, that's the market for you. We often hear about the market averaging around 10 percent over long periods of time. That's true. It just doesn't do it in a nice, linear, stress-free way. It's all over the place. Let's check out the graph in Figure I.2 with the returns by year.

FIGURE I.1

Welcome to the Jungle

---

[1] "Flipping the bird," otherwise known as "flipping you off" and a variety of other things, is a decidedly PG–13 concept. I am assuming you are 13 or that someone older than 17 gave you the book, and that this is not a concept you have never heard before or that you will take too much offense to. Besides, I'm not really flipping you the bird; the market is. I can't control that.

FIGURE I.2

Percentage Change in S&P Market Index by Year

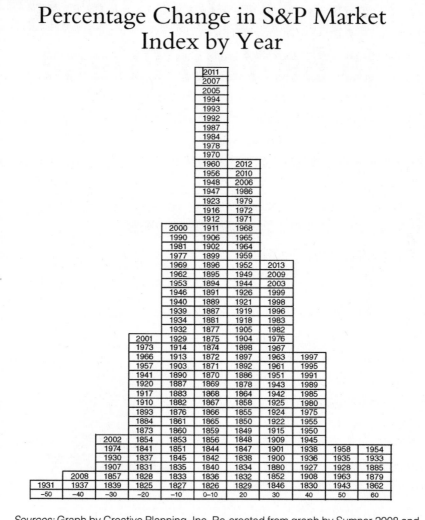

Sources: Graph by Creative Planning, Inc. Re-created from graph by Sumner 2008 and updated with data from S&P Dow Jones Indices, LLC 2014.

So, yes, it is true the market has averaged about a 10 percent return over the long run. However, most investors never get anywhere near that return out of their stock investments. The reason is that the market return varies. A lot. All the time.

This is a concept you need to get comfortable with in order to be a successful investor, as it's a prerequisite to avoiding the mistakes all investors make or are tempted to make, whether it's market timing, actively trading stocks, falling prey to misleading performance data, behavioral mistakes, or not having a solid, disciplined plan.

So what keeps investors from earning the market return? Quite simply, investors prevent themselves from participating in the returns the market wants to give them so easily. *Investors go out of their way to make mistakes that keep them from getting the market return.*

The first step to moving forward is to rid yourself of the misconceptions you may have about what works, to be aware of the most common mistakes and avoid them. That's what this book is about. Recognizing the mistakes to avoid can dramatically improve your investment performance, reduce your stress level, substantially increase the probability you will achieve your investment goals, and even improve the quality of your life.

Let's begin.

Market Timing

B oy, do I have an investment for you! It has earned about 10 percent per year over the last 88 years and has gone straight up. Check it out (see Figure 1.1)!

Now, what if I told you that return was real? More intriguing is that it is readily available to you. It's just waiting for you to participate. What is this incredible, magical investment? Well, it's something you may have heard of: the stock market.

If you are like most Americans, this sort of return seems like a dream. In fact, according to DALBAR, over a 20-year period ending December 31, 2010, the average stock market investor has earned 3.27 percent per year while the S&P 500 Index has returned 9.14 percent. Every time DALBAR repeats their study, the conclusion is the same: Investors' stock portfolio returns regularly lag behind the stock market return by a very wide margin.

Market timing is the idea that there are times to be in the market and times to be out of it. Some people attempt to "protect" their money by exiting the market when they sense a downturn coming or load up on high-risk stocks when they anticipate a recovery.

Let's get one thing straight right out of the box. Market timing doesn't work. It just doesn't. And don't tell me you don't market time either. Have you ever said or thought anything like this:

"I have cash on the sidelines and I am just waiting for things to settle down."

"I have a bonus but I'll wait for a pullback."

"I'll invest after [insert lame excuse here; some choices: the election, the new year, the market corrects, the debt crisis passes, Congress works out the budget, the Cubs win the World Series, or whatever]."

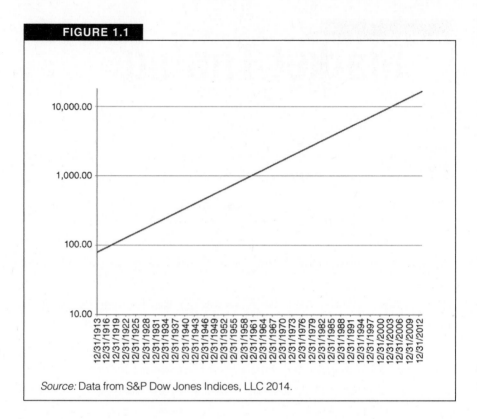

| FIGURE 1.1 |

Source: Data from S&P Dow Jones Indices, LLC 2014.

All of that is market timing.

Why would anyone want to get in the way of an investment that has perpetually produced such fantastical* returns?

Quite simply, it is because the stock market doesn't go up in a straight line. Drawn as the returns actually happened, the graph looks like the one shown in Figure 1.2.

That still doesn't look so bad when we look at it from here, with the full benefit of hindsight. Of course, living through it is a completely different matter. Imagine the emotional turmoil you would have gone through during the Great Depression, the feeling of inertia and futility you would have had to endure through the 1970s, or the panic in 2008 (actually, you likely don't need to imagine that one!). With investing,

---

*Yes, it is a word! "Fantastic" didn't seem adequate enough to describe how great an investment stocks have been.

FIGURE 1.2

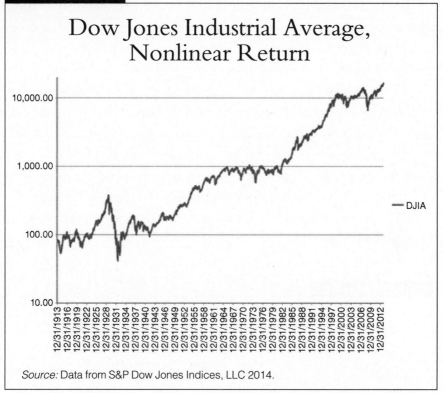

Source: Data from S&P Dow Jones Indices, LLC 2014.

even a few weeks can seem like forever, especially when the market is moving against you.

To be clear, there are many "markets." The graphs we have looked at so far represent the Dow Jones Industrial Average, an index of 30 large U.S. companies with a history allowing us to go back more than 100 years. Today, the more common index is the S&P 500, which is an index of 500 large U.S. companies, like Microsoft, Exxon Mobile, Google, Procter & Gamble, and GE. While there are thousands of stocks, the largest 500 make up about 80 percent of the entire market capitalization. This is because companies like McDonald's, in the S&P 500, are hundreds of times larger than say, the Cheesecake Factory.*

*Clearly, market capitalization is not a reflection on whose desserts are better. More on that later.

Just so no one thinks I am selecting the most awesomest* investment ever as an example, the same holds true for small U.S. stocks, international stocks, and emerging markets stocks. The point being, all broad markets have done the same thing: Go up. A lot.

All of this looks pretty good, right? But to get these returns, you need to avoid making the first big mistake: market timing. This isn't as easy as it sounds because there are lots of people who are encouraging you to make this mistake. Among them are prognosticators on TV, market timers, your buddy at work, your brother-in-law who "jumped out right before the last crash," and the majority of the financial services industry.

This group of market timers can be divided into two camps, as illustrated in Figure 1.3.

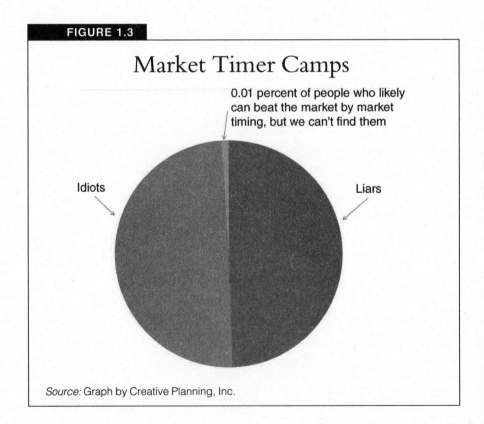

FIGURE 1.3

Market Timer Camps

0.01 percent of people who likely can beat the market by market timing, but we can't find them

Idiots

Liars

Source: Graph by Creative Planning, Inc.

---

*Yes, I realize that this is actually not a word.

Now, that chart isn't scientific. I don't really know what percentage of market timers are incompetent and what percentage are dishonest. I do believe though, that market timers fall into one of these two camps, and both are dangerous. Let's take a look at both groups.

The Idiots

What to do when the market goes down? Read the opinions of the investment gurus who are quoted in the WSJ. And, as you read, laugh. We all know that the pundits can't predict short-term market movements. Yet there they are, desperately trying to sound intelligent when they really haven't got a clue.

—Jonathan Clements

There are perfectly honest investors and advisors who really believe they can time the market. They believe they know something that no one else knows, or that they see something that no one else sees. They often will tell you they got it right before, and maybe they did—once. These folks are often like the friend of yours who tells you "I killed it, baby!" when he returns from Vegas, but conveniently leaves out the five times he lost. They forget their bad decisions and remember their good ones. They may be well intentioned, but ultimately they cause harm to their portfolios and to the portfolios of anyone who listens to them. These folks need to get educated, to learn the folly of their ways. Luckily, you will soon be able to spot these people, avoid them, and maybe even save them from themselves.

The Liars

There are three kinds of people who make market predictions. Those who don't know, those who don't know what they don't know, and those who know darn well they don't know but get big bucks for pretending to know.

—Burton Malkiel*

---

*Burton Malkiel wrote a revolutionary book on this subject called *A Random Walk Down Wallstreet*. He is an advocate of using indexes at the core of a portfolio and active management in certain spaces "around the edges," a philosophy with which I agree.

Unfortunately, many financial advisors know very well that the market can't be timed, but their living depends on convincing you they can "get you out" with their "downside protection." This is the easiest sale in the financial advisory world. *There is nothing a prospective client wants to hear more than the pitch that they can participate in upward movement of the stock market but avoid the pullbacks.* There will always be people who want to hear this, and as long as those people exist, there will be tens of thousands of professionals at the ready to sell them snake oil.

I have also found that many financial advisors have been exposed to all the information they need to change their point of view away from market timing, but a big paycheck makes it hard to accept the facts. Much like a cult member finding definitive proof their founder is a fraud, the financial advisor can find the reality too much to accept and simply remain delusional and ignorant. As Descarte said, "Man is incapable of understanding any argument that interferes with his revenue."[*]

The prognosticators in the media also are eager to give you big, bold market calls. I have been on several national business channels, including CNBC and FOX Business. Prior to the show, the producer always asks me for my thoughts on "where the market is going." They are disappointed every time when I answer that over the short run "I don't know." That doesn't make for the most exciting guest in the world. One national cable network even branded me "The Time Machine" advisor because I kept prefacing my advice by saying I had no idea what would happen in the short run but was very confident about the long run. The graphics were quite amusing with my head sticking outside of a time machine that looked mainly like an old-school phone booth.[†]

In short, if you want to get clients and be on TV, the easiest path is to sell market timing. The financial services industry rewards the deliberate delivery of misinformation.

---

[*] Also a very smart guy, but reading his books will teach you nothing about investing.

[†] My brother-in-law will never let me forget it.

Why Is It So Hard to Beat the Market?

In an efficient market, at any point in time, the actual price of a security will be a good estimate of its intrinsic value.

—Eugene Fama

There are many reasons market timing fails to work, and there are many reasons investment managers will try to tell you they can do it. Let's start by looking at the big picture, then work our way through the investment gurus and their actual results.

Efficient Markets

The efficient market hypothesis was developed by Nobel Laureate Eugene Fama. This investment theory can be summed up like this: It's tough to beat the market because markets are efficient at incorporating all relevant information. Since a bunch of smart people (and not so smart people) all know the same thing about any given security, it is impossible to have a sustainable edge that will allow you to beat the market return.

Where there appear to be patterns that the market can be beat, it is almost always due to the investor taking on additional risk. For example, there is evidence that small company stocks perform better than large company stocks over long periods of time, and this is very likely because they are riskier (more volatile).

While it is not my point of view that the markets are perfectly efficient, the evidence is fairly overwhelming that it is efficient enough to kick a market timer's butt.* Regardless, it gives us a premise from which all the rest of the evidence will follow.

Being a Little Better Than the Market Isn't Good Enough

Why is it so difficult to go in and out of the market repeatedly with success? The problem is that many investors think you simply need to be

---

* Technically speaking.

right more than 50 percent of the time, when in fact, an exhaustive study by Nobel Laureate William Sharpe* definitively concluded that the investor must be right 69 to 91 percent of the time, depending on market moves (Sharpe 1975). Good luck with that.

The Evidence (Research and Stuff)

The evidence against market timing is overwhelming.

This brings us to a comprehensive study by Richard Bauer and Julie Dahlquist (2001). In what may be the most exhaustive study ever done on market timing, the researchers examined over 1 million market timing sequences from 1926 to 1999. The conclusion: Holding the market outperformed over 80 percent of market timing strategies (Bauer and Dahlquist 2001, p. 38). That's a lot of scenarios run over a long period of time with one overwhelming conclusion. That doesn't seem to square with what many people do, what we hear from the masses, the media, economists, investment managers, newsletters, and your friends. Let's look at each.

The Masses Get It Wrong, Over and Over Again

We do not have an opinion about where the stock market, interest rates, or business activity will be a year from now. We've long felt the only value of stock forecasts is to make fortune tellers look good. We believe that short-term market forecasts are poison and should be kept locked up in a safe place, away from children and also from grown-ups who behave in the market like children.

—Warren Buffett

For the average investor, there has been spectacular mistiming of the market. At the bottom of the 2001 bear market, investors moved a then record amount of their money from stocks to cash. They then re-entered the market when it recovered. At the bottom of the 2008/2009 crisis, investors broke the record for stock market withdrawals, moving their money to cash in record numbers. Today, the market is up over

---

*Yes, at some point we will cite people who aren't Nobel Laureates.

100 percent from those levels. Investors had mistimed the market perfectly, breaking records both ways, both times at exactly the wrong time.

The Media Get It Wrong, Over and Over Again

The typical investor is getting their financial information from the media. It's important to note that the total sum value of all the information provided from the media regarding market calls is zero. Actually, it is less than zero because if you follow the guidance of the media on market calls, you are likely going to create a negative, rather than a neutral, result. Let's take a look at some examples:

"The Death of Equities." August 13, 1979, *BusinessWeek*—just prior to the biggest stock market run up in history.

"The Crash. . . . After a wild week on Wall Street, the world is different." November 11, 1987, *Time*—the market proceeded to rocket 31 percent over the next 12 months.

"Buy Stocks. No Way!" September 26, 1988, *Time*—just before the greatest 10-year run in market history.

"Will you be able to retire? With stocks plummeting and corporations in disarray, American's financial futures are in peril." July 29, 2002, *Time*—the market was up 21 percent from July 2002 through June 2003.

The media's job is not to inform you; it is to get eyeballs. Eyeballs lead to advertising revenue. That means they need people to read stuff and view stuff. Telling everyone things are going to work out just fine doesn't get eyeballs the way feeding into fear does. That doesn't just explain financial news; it explains most of the news.

Economists Get It Wrong, Over and Over Again

If you are going to predict, predict often.

—John Kenneth Gailbraith

Forecasts may tell you a great deal about the forecaster, but they tell you nothing about the future.

—Warren Buffett

He who predicts the future lies, even if he tells the truth.

—Proverbs

Economists have shown no ability to predict the direction of the economy. There are simply too many variables, many known and some unknown, for anyone to do so with any sort of sustainable accuracy. History provides us with two great anecdotes to this point. On October 15, 1929, Irving Fisher, whom Milton Friedman declared the "greatest economist the United States has ever produced," asserted that "stock prices have reached what looks like a permanently high plateau." The following week, the market crashed, taking us into the Great Depression and beginning a free fall that would eventually see the Dow lose 88 percent of its value. It would be nearly 80 years before another stock market fall would come close to that one. Of course, there was a high profile economist making a bold prediction just prior to the turmoil. On January 10, 2008, Ben Bernanke stated "the Federal Reserve is currently not forecasting a recession."* Unfortunately, the economy didn't listen, as a few months later the economy slid into the worst recession since the Great Depression, taking the stock market down more than 50 percent along the way.

Some economists have gained quite a bit of notoriety with their bold predictions. Bolder, it seems, is better. Harry Dent has become a quite popular economist despite his wildly unsuccessful market calls. It seems the more hyperbolic the predictions, the more attention he garners. In his 2006 book, *The Next Great Bubble Boom*, Dent wrote, "The Dow Jones Industrial Average could reach as high as 35,000 or 40,000 by late 2008 or 2009. . . . This continues to be our forecast . . ." (Dent 2006, p. 44). Of

---

*Now, ponder this for a moment. The Federal Reserve is arguably run by the best economic team on Earth. If they can't predict what is going to happen, and they control interest rates which drive at least part of what happens, how are you, your buddy, or your financial guy going to predict what happens?

course, we all know that the market fell into free fall in what turned out to be the greatest pullback since the Great Depression, bottoming in March of 2009. Almost stunning in its unfortunate timing, Dent came out with a new book in, you guessed it, 2009 called *The Great Depression Ahead* (Dent 2008). In this book, Dent predicted that the recession would become a depression and the Dow Jones Industrial Average would drop to 3,800. He strongly advocated that investors take any 2009 bounce in the market to sell all of their stocks and real estate and move to cash. This would be funny if it weren't so sad. Dent relentlessly promoted these books and was given a podium on financial networks to promote his forecasts. Both books were best sellers. Unfortunately, anyone following the "Boom" book went in at the wrong time and much, much worse, anyone following the "Depression" book sold out at the worst possible time.

In advertisements in May 2013 on his *Survive & Prosper* website Dent wrote, "I see the Dow Jones Average winding down, week after week . . . before ultimately dropping as low as 3,300. And there's nothing you or I, or any politician or government, or any team of monetary experts can do to stop the Dow Jones Index from dropping. . . . But here's the good news, extraordinary wealth can be made by knowing the future. In *Survive & Prosper*, my free e-letter, I'll show you my economic analysis and demographic research that proves the DOW is about to make a historic drop. . . . I will show how predicting and profiting from the future is a SCIENCE and is easier than you might have imagined" (Dent 2013). This guy, like just about everyone selling their ability to time the market, is nothing but a charlatan.

Despite making spectacularly wrong prediction after spectacularly wrong prediction, AIM partnered with him to start a mutual fund tracking his advice, the "AIM Dent Demographic Trends Fund." It quickly gathered $2 billion in assets, largely due to the publicity that surrounds Dent. It quickly lost 80 percent of its assets due to terrible performance. Dent said it was due to the fund not taking all of his advice. Dent may have a harder time explaining the performance of the "Dent ETF," which was launched on September 9, 2009, and was run by "HS

Dent Investment Management" until they resigned on June 2, 2012. On his website, www.hsdent.com, Dent calls his methodology "the ultimate economic forecasting tool for asset protection and growth" (Roth 2012). So how did the ETF perform while he managed it? During their tenure, it lost 12.9 percent. Over the same time period, the U.S. market was up 42.7 percent and the bond market was up 18.2 percent. It is very difficult to lose this much money during a bull market. It's almost impossible to do, even if you try. Despite being so wrong so many times, Dent still has his followers and gets plenty of media airplay. Extreme predictions have no problem finding airwaves.

Most economists cannot forecast the market correctly, and the evidence bears that out. However, occasionally, an economist does make what appears to be an accurate forecast. One such economist is the now famous Dr. Nouriel Roubini, the Chairman of Roubini Global Economics. Roubini, now known as the ominous "Dr. Doom,"* warned the public about the coming recession prior to it occurring. However, according to the Economic Predictions Research Project as published on the Wall Street Economists Institute website, Dr. Doom actually predicted a recession in 2004 (incorrectly), 2005 (oops, no recession), 2006 (sorry, still no recession), and 2007 (you guessed it, still no recession). If you followed Dr. Doom's advice, yes, you would have been out of the market prior to the 2008 drop, but you also would have been out of it for the four years prior and a few years after. All in all, you would have far less money following Dr. Doom's predictions than had you done nothing!

At an International Monetary Fund meeting in 2006, Dr. Doom was quoted as saying:

> My analysis has been based on circumstantial kind of observations. . . . I
> said the probability of a recession is "70 percent." If you ask me where I

---

*You have officially hit it big as an economist when you have a nickname. Dr. Roubini is Dr. Doom. Marc Faber, another high-profile doomsday permabear, also has a nickname. It's also Dr. Doom. It seems that the longer and louder you are about how bad things are about to get, the more likely you will get a nickname, albeit not an original one.

got that number: just out of my nose,* I will be very honest about that. I think if you would have said "50 percent" you would look like a wimp, it means you are not sure. So if you have the guts of believing there is going to be a recession, you should say something higher than that, and that is where the "70 percent" comes from. So my model is like a "smell test. . . ."

—NYT *Roubini Article, IMF Transcript*

Translation: Dr. Doom, perhaps the most celebrated economic forecaster of our time, is basically saying his guesses are based on a "smell test" and he inflates his hunches to appear more confident.

I can't make this stuff up. Seriously!

Again, it would be funny if the financial media didn't elevate him and let his opinions about market movements carry such weight and go unchallenged. If a viewer saw Dr. Doom explain his outlook while the financial network showed his former predictions alongside a running ticker, perhaps he wouldn't carry quite the weight he does, and instead elicit an eye roll. Unfortunately, all people hear is that Dr. Doom predicted the 2008 recession and then listen carefully, and often act upon, his newer, ominous (as is almost always the case) predictions.

Now, I know what you're thinking: "Well, Dr. Doom might be the most famous economist to predict the crisis, but his failure to correctly predict almost anything else isn't indicative of economic forecasters in general."† Well, thanks for bringing that point up. Let's take a look at the entire field of economic forecasters who, like Harry Dent and Dr. Doom, make strong predictions.

Fortunately, I don't need to spend time researching to figure this out. Oxford economist Jerker Denrell and Christina Fang of New York University looked at all the predictions in the *Wall Street Journal*'s Survey of Economic Forecasts from July 2002 through July 2005 (Denrell and Fang 2010). They then narrowed their search to isolate the group of

---

*My personal opinion is that he got it right out of somewhere else.

†Or you could be thinking, "Hey, it's time for a sandwich break." Hey, I'm not a mind reader!

economists who had proven to be the most successful at predicting unlikely outcomes. To do this, they defined an "extreme" prediction as one in which the economist's outlook was either 20 percent higher or 20 percent lower than the average prediction. Now, these economists appear to be darn good at predicting things. After all, they are taking positions where they stand alone, or in the minority, and have been proven right.

Well, not so much. Denrell and Fang then looked at the other predictions of this group and found that these economists, the ones with the best success rate at predicting "extreme" events, actually had a *worse* record overall. In other words, the more crazy the prediction an economist makes, the more likely he is to hit a home run every now and then, but the more likely he is to strike out far more than normal. Is this the type of person you want to get investment advice from?

Here's the deal: The more certain a forecaster is of their prediction, the less likely they are to be right, and the more likely their prediction is a derivative of showmanship. When it comes to investing, the bolder the prediction, the less valid the source. If you care about your financial well being, the data strongly suggests you would be far better off ignoring it.

Joe Stiglitz, a Nobel Prize–winning economist,* has said that economists get it right "about 3 or 4 times out of 10" (Weber 2011). With those odds, I'll pass. You should too.

Investment Managers Get It Wrong, Over and Over Again

Sure it would be great to get out of the stock market at the high and back in at the low, but in 55 years in the business, I not only have never met anybody that knew how to do it, I've never met anybody who had met anybody that knew how to do it.
—John Bogle, founder of Vanguard

There are literally thousands, if not tens of thousands, of financial advisors claiming to have "market indicators" that help them time the

---

*Here we go again with the Nobel Prize guys.

market. The most well-known among this group is Ken Fisher. Ken is one of the largest investment managers in America and a popular *Forbes* columnist. He claims to be able to beat the market by "identifying information not widely known" by others, according to Fisher Investments Philosophy. While Ken uses direct marketing and a legion of marketing representatives to promote his private portfolio management service, they rarely mention the publicly available mutual fund they run. The Purisima Total Return Fund consists of securities chosen by Ken and his team, presumably following his tried and tested strategy for success. According to Morningstar, through January 1, 2014, this fund ranks below average in its peer group over every time period: 1 year, 3 years, 5 years, 10 years, and since inception.

In September 2007, Ken wrote in his column: "This is a phony credit crunch . . . a few months from now we will be wondering what the fuss was about" (Fisher 2007). Perhaps Ken's boldest prediction came in January 2008, as the market began its downward spiral. Ken wrote in his column: "Let me make you a solemn promise for 2008 . . . America should do well in 2008—better, at any rate, than people expect. . . . My advice is to stay fully invested on a global basis, with stocks like these. . . ." (Fisher 2008).

Of course, what followed was the biggest single calendar year loss the stock market had seen since the Great Depression, and in 2008 the Purisma Fund run by Fisher's team was down 42.95 percent, far worse than the S&P 500.

Let's be clear though—while Ken Fisher is one of the biggest market timers, he is not alone in his inability to consistently time the market correctly, or even enough to outperform. As Don Phillips, the managing director of Morningstar said: "I can't point to any mutual fund anywhere in the world that's produced a superior long-term record using market timing as its main investment criteria" (Britton 2011).

While Ken Fisher was wrong about 2008, Peter Schiff nailed it. As early as December of 2006, investment advisor Peter Schiff predicted the coming economic crisis. However, the Economic Predictions Research Project as published on the Wall Street Economists Institute website puts that in context. Below is a list of Peter Schiff's major predictions from 2002 through 2012:

May, 2002—The DOW will drop to 4,000—DID NOT HAPPEN.

December 16, 2006—Interest rates and inflation will go higher—DID NOT HAPPEN.

December 16, 2006—There will be inflation in 2008 and 2009—DID NOT HAPPEN.

December 16, 2006—U.S. equities will crash—HAPPENED! This is the prediction he is known for getting "right."

Predicted repeatedly prior and during the crisis: Buy foreign equities and commodities—DID NOT HAPPEN and a big "oops." It turns out that while he was right about the U.S. market, his solution was not so right. Foreign equities actually sold off far more than U.S. stocks, down over 43 percent. Peter Schiff invested his clients per his recommendations and they sustained the brunt of the crash.

January 16, 2009—At a minimum, the dollar will lose another 40 to 50 percent in 2010—DID NOT HAPPEN.

January 2, 2009—U.S. stocks are heading a lot lower in 2009, 2010, and 2011.—DID NOT HAPPEN—over this time period, U.S. stocks were up approximately over 40 percent!

September 9, 2009—Gold will go to $5,000—DID NOT HAPPEN.

September 9, 2009—U.S. dollars will go close to zero—DID NOT HAPPEN.

January 12, 2010—Buy commodities like gold—HAPPENED, except they later crashed with his clients still in the asset class.

August 26, 2010—We probably won't make it to 2012—DID NOT HAPPEN.

December 31, 2010—U.S. markets will crash like dominos and many bad things are bound to happen in 2011—DID NOT HAPPEN.

To sum it up, Peter Schiff did make a major market prediction, *but* his solution didn't work and most of his other predictions have been dead wrong. I concur with Todd Sullivan of Seeking Alpha, who wrote "had you placed bets on Schiff's market calls, you lost everything you wagered" (Sullivan 2008).

The bottom line is this: There are tens of thousands of investment managers who claim to be able to market time. Some are famous and some are not. They all have one thing in common though: None of them can do this effectively and repeatedly. The odds of getting it right over time are extremely low, and only a fool would play such a game with the markets. An even bigger fool would pay someone else to gamble with their money this way. The odds are so stacked against the market timer that any long-term outcome other than colossal failure is rarely avoidable.*

Newsletters Get It Wrong, Over and Over Again

The only way to make money with a newsletter is by selling one.

—Malcolm Forbes

Tens of thousands of Americans subscribe to a variety of market timing newsletters. These Americans are paying a fee and spending a lot of time to increase their chances of underperforming the market.

In 1994, John Graham and Campbell Harvey, analyzing data provided by Mark Hulbert,† conducted what many consider the most comprehensive study on the ability of newsletters to predict the market (Graham and Harvey 1994). They looked at over 15,000 market timing calls from 237 newsletters over 13 years. The conclusion was overwhelming: 75 percent of the newsletters produced negative abnormal returns. Basically, following the advice of most of these letters created negative performance!

Some of the newsletters, like the once famous *Granville Market Letter*, produced an average negative annual return of 5.4 percent. The *Elliot*

---

*Rule #1 of investing: Avoid colossal failure. Colossal failure is bad.

†Mark Hulbert runs a service that tracks newsletter predictions and performance.

Wave Theorist letter, a favorite of doomsday fanatics, produced a negative annual return of 14.8 percent.* During the same time period the S&P 500 earned 15.9 percent per year, outperforming a full three-quarters of the newsletters.

You might ask, well what about the one-quarter that did match or beat the market? It seems impossible, but the study actually overstates the performance of market timing newsletters. Had the study accounted for fees, transaction costs, and taxes, the underperformance would have been even worse! Finally, the authors took their study further, checking to see if winners keep on winning. The conclusion is clear: "Winners rarely win again."

The authors are harsh and definitive in the conclusion of their study, saying "There is no evidence that the letters can time the market."

Mark Hulbert's own research shows that the few that do outperform the market in any given year are not the same in future years (Snider 2014). In other words, a good year has no predictive value looking forward. His data on market timing letters specifically provides an even more dismal outlook: His data shows that not a single market timing newsletter has beaten the market over the long run (Snider 2014)!

Your Buddy

Only liars manage to always be out during bad times and in during good times.
—Bernard Baruch

Of course, we all know that one guy—the one who "had a feeling" about when to get out of the market.† He is like your buddy who tells you about the times he won in Vegas but forgets to include all the times he lost. There is no doubt that some people get some market calls right.

---

* Isn't it interesting how the doomsday fanatics end up losing their money despite their desperate attempts to save it?

† Your buddy says stuff like this: "Dude, the market is so overvalued. Anyone can see that!" or "The charts made it so easy to know when to get out before the last correction."

There will always be people who do. However, in order to be successful, they need to be right about when to get out *and* when to move back into the market. More importantly, they need to do this *repeatedly*. In all likelihood, the person who got it right this time has tried it many times in the past, and will continue to do so in the future. *The odds are extremely high this person will ultimately fail.* In my entire career, I have personally never seen an investor exit the market near a top and enter it again near a bottom. Not once. And whoever does do it needs to do it over and over to succeed. Do you really think your buddy can do something even the pros can't do? The statistics, the probabilities, and not to mention plain old common sense, say no.

Strategies That Don't Sound Like Market Timing but Are Market Timing—Oh, and They Don't Work, Either

If you are ever talking with an advisor who tells you he doesn't market time, ask some further questions. Often, they will try to sell you what you want to hear, which is market timing, but packaged in a different way. They will say things like "downside protection," "asset-class rotation," "tactical allocation," "style rotation," and "sector rotation." They will say all sorts of things that imply they can regularly predict when to move from one part of the market to another. All of this is market timing and the evidence is overwhelming that it does not work.

Asset-Class Rotation

An asset-class rotation strategy attempts to select the ideal time to move from one asset class to another. The "sale" here is usually "downside protection." When marketed, advisors often sell the idea they will own stocks while the market is going up, but will shift to cash before it goes down. In his 1984 article, "The Folly of Stock Market Timing," Robert Jeffrey examined annual switches between stocks and cash and concluded "the potential downside from market timing exceeds the potential upside by a wide margin" (Jeffrey 1984).

Going forward, any time you hear "asset-class rotation" or "downside protection strategy" your BS meter should be beeping loudly.*

Tactical Asset Allocation

Tactical asset allocation funds attempt to beat the market by moving from one broad asset class to another. In February 2012, Morningstar compared 210 tactical asset allocation portfolios against a 60 percent stock/ 40 percent bond Vanguard portfolio. The conclusion: "With a few exceptions, they gained less, were more volatile, or were subject to just as much downside risk as a 60 percent/40 percent mix of U.S. stocks and bonds" (Ptak 2012). In other words, tactical allocation provides a wilder ride for a lesser return.† No thank you!

Style Rotation

With this strategy, an advisor is selling the idea they can move from one style of investing to another at optimal times. Common style rotation strategies include moving from value stocks to growth stocks or attempting to move from large dividend paying stocks to small stocks at the right times. Same deal—the evidence supports that this doesn't work.

Sector Rotation

A sector rotation strategy promises outperformance by moving from one sector to another at the right time. For example, a money manager may move from financial stocks to health care stocks, depending on where they see the economy going. Again, this is just market timing under another name and the evidence is this doesn't work either.

----

*If you haven't noticed, part of being successful at investing is having a really good BS meter. We are talking really advanced. Off the shelf won't do it. There's just too much BS out there to survive without anything but the best.
† The irony of these strategies is that they often create more volatility and deliver a lesser return, which is the exact opposite of what the investor is attempting to accomplish.

What Smart Investors Have to Say on Market Timing

The market timing Hall of Fame is an empty room.

Jane Bryant Quinn

Among the great investors of all time, none of them advocate market timing. J. P. Morgan, who dominated finance in his time, was asked by a young investor what the market would do. J. P. Morgan replied, "It will fluctuate, young man. It will fluctuate." Benjamin Graham, the father of modern investing, advocated against market timing, saying in 1976, "If I have learned anything over these 60 years on Wall Street, it is that people do not succeed in forecasting what is going to happen in the stock market." John Bogle, the founder of Vanguard, the largest fund company in the world, has said repeatedly that he finds market timing impossible and futile. Warren Buffett, who has been peerless in modern-day investing, has mocked market timing repeatedly, often citing it as simply the stupidest thing an investor can do. He has many thoughts on the subject including "Forecasters exist to make fortune tellers look good" and, more to the point, "I have *never* met a man that can time the market."

Knowing All This, Why Would Anyone Market Time?

Wall Street never changes, the pockets change, the suckers change, the stocks change, but Wall Street never changes, because human nature never changes.

—Jesse Livermore

Knowing that media, economists, newsletters, investment managers, and just about everyone else has not effectively timed the market, and having seen what legendary investors have to say about market timing, why would anyone try to time the market? Reasons for both the investor and "professional" selling market timing are the same: ignorance, greed, or both. Investors want to believe there is someone who can get in before the market goes up and get out before it goes down. None of the other investment strategies, even if they can lessen losses or increase gains, sound nearly as appealing. And if people want it, someone will sell it and try to keep a straight face doing so. To make it easier to sneak by you, the advisor may not call it market timing, but instead use code for market timing. Upton Sinclair once said: "It is difficult to get a man to understand something when his salary depends on not understanding it." For as long as we are alive, there will be thousands of advisors selling market timing. You can count on it.

To survive market turmoil without getting pulled into the market timing mistake, one must understand the frequency of major market moves, especially corrections and bear markets.

Corrections

Far more money has been lost by investors preparing for corrections, or trying to anticipate corrections, than has been lost in corrections themselves. . . .

—Peter Lynch

A stock market correction is coming. Guaranteed.

That is quite a statement since I just spent a few thousand words talking about how market timing is practically impossible. So, how can I make such a prediction? I can make it because stock market corrections happen all the time. They are a given. Predicting one is like saying, "It is going to rain sometime this year."

Let us start with the definition of a "correction." It is simply a stock market drop of 10 percent or more. If the market drops a total of 20 percent, we change the name from correction to "bear market."

How frequently does a correction occur? Using the year 1900 as a starting point, corrections happen approximately every year. This means if you are around age 55 and reading this letter, you can plan on experiencing about 30 or more corrections.

Why not get out of the market once it drops 10 percent to avoid a further drop into bear market territory? The reason is that most corrections never officially become bear markets. Historically, the average correction is a drop of 13.5 percent. Most corrections last less than two months, with the average length of a correction sitting at just 54 days. Less than one in five corrections turns into an official bear market.

Knowing this, it does not make sense to go to cash whenever a correction occurs. In fact, with odds like that, it is a rather illogical decision to convert to cash once the market drops 10 percent. You would basically be moving to cash right before the typical bottom. Imagine how badly you could screw up your portfolio if you reacted to even a few of these corrections.

Predicting stock market corrections and bear markets is a sport of sorts. To make matters more difficult, sometimes corrections happen for a reason and sometimes they do not.

We know it is a fact that corrections happen all the time. We know that most corrections do not evolve into bear markets. We also know that every single correction in history has given way to a full recovery. It seems completely ridiculous to panic and go to cash. The math is against you, the evidence is against you, and the natural bias of the market is against you—all three are going to get together and do serious damage to your portfolio.

It is fun, however, to watch market prognosticators make themselves look spectacularly silly predicting a correction. Figure 1.4 shows just a small sampling of predictions from the pros during a recent two-year period—the market refused to correct for them, despite their confident proclamations. Enjoy.

The following are some corresponding market prognosticators' correction predictions from Figure 1.4:

1. "Market Correction Ahead," Bert Dohmen, Dohmen Capital Research Group, March 7, 2012

2. "Stocks Flirt with Correction," Ben Rooney, *CNNMoney*, June 1, 2012

3. "10 percent Market Correction Looms: Dig In or Bail Out?" Matt Krantz, *USA Today*, June 5, 2012

4. "A significant equity-price correction could, in fact, be the force that in 2013 tips the US economy into outright contraction," Nouriel Roubini, Roubini Global Economics, July 20, 2012

FIGURE 1.4

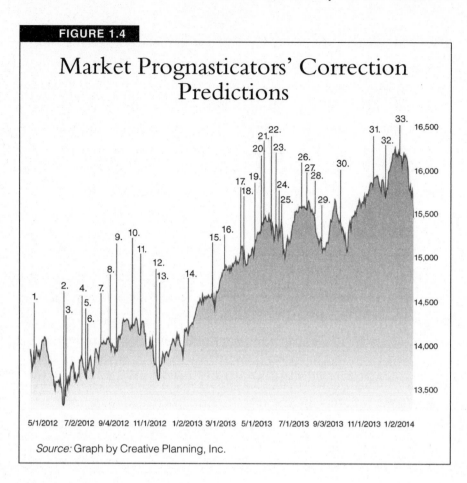

Market Prognasticators' Correction Predictions

Source: Graph by Creative Planning, Inc.

5. "Prepare for Stock Market Crash 2013," Jonathan Yates, money-morning.com, July 23, 2012

6. "Dr. Doom 2013 Prediction: Roubini Says Worse Global Economic Turmoil Approaching; Five Factors to Blame," Kukil Bora, *International Business Times*, July 24, 2012

7. "Watch Out for a Correction—or Worse," Mark Hulbert, MarketWatch, August 8, 2012

8. "We think we are set up for an 8–10 percent correction in the month of September," MaryAnn Bartels, Bank of America Merrill Lynch, August 22, 2012

 9. "It's Coming: One Pro Sees Big Stock Selloff in 10 Days," John Melloy, CNBC, September 4, 2012

10. "Warning: Stock Correction May Be Coming," Hibah Yousuf, *CNNMoney*, October 4, 2012

11. "I'm going around town telling my hedge fund clients that the U.S. economy is headed into recession," Michael Belkin, Belkin Limited, October 15, 2012

12. "Fiscal Cliff Blues May Lead to Correction," Caroline Valetkevitch and Ryan Vlastelica, Reuters, November 9, 2012

13. "Why a Severe Stock Market Correction's Imminent," Mitchell Clark, Lombardi Financial, November 14, 2012

14. "By summer, we get another crash," Harry Dent, Dent Research, January 8, 2013

15. "A Stock Market Correction May Have Begun," Rick Newman, *U.S. News*, February 21, 2013

16. "Sluggish Economy May Signal Correction," Maureen Farrell, CNNMoney.com, February 28, 2013

17. "I think a correction is coming," Byron Wein, Blackstone, April 4, 2013

18. "Markets Long Overdue Correction Seems to Be Starting," Jonathan Castle, Paragon Wealth Strategies, April 8, 2013

19. "5 Warning Signs of a Coming Market Correction," Dawn Bennett, Bennett Group Financial Services, April 16, 2013

20. "Stock Market Warning Signs Becoming Ominous," Sy Harding, StreetSmartReport.com, April 22, 2013

21. "Don't buy—sell risk assets," Bill Gross, PIMCO, May 2, 2013

22. "This may not be the time to sprint away from risk, but it is the time to walk away," Mohamed El-Erian, PIMCO, May 22, 2013

23. "We're due for a correction soon," Byron Wein, Blackstone, June 3, 2013

24. "Doomsday Poll: 87 Percent Risk of Stock Crash by Year-End," Paul Farrell, MarketWatch, June 5, 2013

25. "Stock Shrink: Market Heading for Severe Correction," Adam Shell, *USA Today*, June 15, 2013

26. "Don't Be Complacent—A Market Correction Is On Its Way," Sasha Cekerevac, Investment Contrarians, July 12, 2013

27. "For Two Months, My Models Have Told Me That July 19th Would be the start of a Big Stock Market Sell-Off," Jeff Saut, Raymond James, July 18, 2013

28. "Signs of a Market Correction Ahead," John Kimelman, *Barron's*, August 13, 2013

29. "Correction Watch: How Soon? How Bad? How to Prepare?" Kevin Cook, Zacks.com, August 23, 2013

30. "I Think There's a Decent Chance Stocks Will Crash," Henry Blodget, *Business Insider*, September 26, 2013

31. "5 Reasons to Expect a Correction," Jeff Reeves, *MarketWatch*, November 18, 2013

32. "Time to Brace for a 20 Percent Correction," Richard Rescigno, *Barron's*, December 14, 2013

33. "Blackstone's Wien: Stock Market Poised for 10 Percent Correction," Dan Weil, Moneynews.com, January 16, 2014

Bear Markets: An Overview

The key to making money in equities is to not get scared out of them.

—Peter Lynch

A bear market is coming. Guaranteed.

I know, I know. I just said that about corrections. Well, it's true about bear markets too. Bear markets don't happen nearly as frequently as corrections, but they also happen all the time. A bear market is defined as a stock market decline of 20 percent or more.* Bear markets occur every

---

*Ten percent and 20 percent are just numbers, but in real life, when experienced, they elicit quite different reactions. If a correction feels unsettling to you, a bear market will make you want to curl up in a ball and cry for Mommy.

FIGURE 1.5

Bear Markets: How Often, How Long, and How Severe?

Bull Market Top	Bear Market Bottom	Number of Days Duration	% Decline in S&P 500
05/29/1946	05/17/1947	353	−23.2%
04/06/1956	10/22/1957	564	−19.4%
12/13/1961	06/26/1962	195	−27.1%
02/09/1966	10/07/1966	240	−25.2%
12/03/1968	05/26/1970	539	−35.9%
01/11/1973	12/06/1974	694	−45.1%
09/21/1976	02/28/1978	525	−26.9%
04/27/1981	08/12/1982	472	−24.1%
08/25/1987	12/04/1987	101	−33.5%
07/16/1990	10/11/1990	87	−21.2%
07/17/1998	08/31/1998	45	−19.3%
03/24/2000	09/21/2001	547	−36.8%
01/04/2002	07/23/2002	210	−32.0%
10/11/2007	03/09/2009	512	−57.6%

three to five years, depending on how far back you want to look. There have been 34 bear markets from 1900 to 2014, including 14 since 1946. The four bear markets from 2000 on have been jarring for investors with all sorts of crises assaulting the markets. The average bear market decline is 33 percent and more than one-third of bear markets have suffered drops over 40 percent. The average bear market lasts close to a year with almost all of them lasting anywhere between eight months and two years (see Figure 1.5).

Bear Markets Happen for Different Reasons, but the Outcome Is Always the Same

The four most expensive words in the English language are: "This time it's different."

—John Templeton

Bear markets occur when a lot of people think things are going to be really bad for a really long time. If we know that every bear market has given way to a bull market, then why would anyone ever panic and go to cash? The reason is that each bear market tends to happen for a different reason than the one before it. Looking at recent bear markets, we have everything from a computer-driven crash, to a tech bubble, to a terrorist event and war, to a liquidity crisis. Because each drop is driven by a different set of facts, investors panic thinking that in fact, "This time is different." While the actual set of facts driving the bear market may be different, the outcome is always the same: The economy finds a way to move on. Every single time. No exceptions. The next time we go through a bear market, remind yourself of all the things we have been through in the past 80 years. If the economy can survive all of this, it can likely get through the next bear market:

1940s World War II

1960s/1970s Vietnam War

1970/1980s Hyperinflation

1970s/1980s Commodity Crisis

1980s Real Estate and Banking Collapse

1980s Emerging Markets Crisis

1987 Flash Crash

1990s Asian Contagion Crisis

2000 Tech Bubble Bursts

2001 9/11 Attack and Subsequent Afghanistan and Iraq Wars

2008/2009 Liquidity Crisis

Figure 1.6 shows what it looks like against the market.

And keep in mind that the previous list is by no means all inclusive. There are many distractions along the way that will cause prognosticators to predict the next bear, whether it is a downgrade of the United States, a "fiscal cliff," a budget debate, an election, or whatever happens to be the news cycle of the day.

FIGURE 1.6

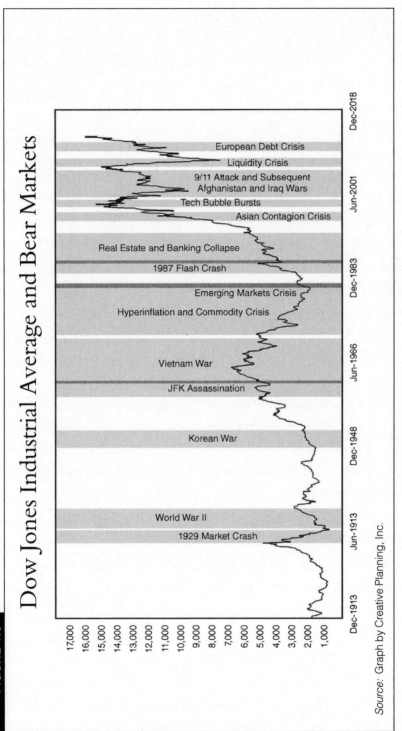

Dow Jones Industrial Average and Bear Markets

European Debt Crisis

Liquidity Crisis

9/11 Attack and Subsequent
Afghanistan and Iraq Wars

Tech Bubble Bursts

Asian Contagion Crisis

Real Estate and Banking Collapse

1987 Flash Crash

Emerging Markets Crisis

Hyperinflation and Commodity Crisis

Vietnam War

JFK Assassination

Korean War

World War II

1929 Market Crash

17,000
16,000
15,000
14,000
13,000
12,000
11,000
10,000
9,000
8,000
7,000
6,000
5,000
4,000
3,000
2,000
1,000

Dec-1913 Jun-1913 Dec-1948 Jun-1966 Dec-1983 Jun-2001 Dec-2018

Source: Graph by Creative Planning, Inc.

Bear Markets Are Not Predictable

Here's the thing though: Bear markets are not predictable. No one on earth has consistently and repeatedly predicted bear markets. Remember, to exploit a bear market, you need to know when to get out, know when to get back in, and then do it again. I can't find the guy who's done that. You're not going to find him either. He's Santa Claus. You might want to think he exists, for a while you believe he exists, there comes a point where you know enough to know he doesn't exist but you can't admit it yourself, and then finally, maybe you will accept it. Also like Santa Claus, there are a lot of people running around pretending to be that guy you want to believe in so badly.*

When Bear Markets "Turn," They Make People on the Sidelines Look Silly

Now, you might acknowledge that you can't possibly get out and back correctly and repeatedly, but you may be thinking: "I'll at least get out and wait for things to settle, miss a small part of the recovery, then jump back in." This too, is likely not possible. When bear markets give way to bull markets, they often first have several false starts, but when they "turn" for real, *they tend to do so quickly and furiously*, leaving most market timers sitting with their hands firmly under their derrières. Figure 1.7 illustrates this point.

The Market Is Volatile—Get Used to It

You get recessions. You get market declines. If you don't understand that is going to happen, then you won't do well in the markets.

—Peter Lynch

Sometimes a year goes by without a correction or bear market. Sometimes the market ends the year with a solid return, and in the

---

*I am pretty sure that with the book's opening graph, I eliminated the chance of anyone reading this book who still believes in Santa Claus.

FIGURE 1.7

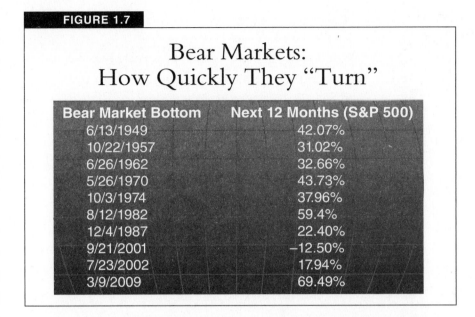

Bear Markets:
How Quickly They "Turn"

Bear Market Bottom	Next 12 Months (S&P 500)
6/13/1949	42.07%
10/22/1957	31.02%
6/26/1962	32.66%
5/26/1970	43.73%
10/3/1974	37.96%
8/12/1982	59.4%
12/4/1987	22.40%
9/21/2001	−12.50%
7/23/2002	17.94%
3/9/2009	69.49%

rearview mirror it looks easy. That is very rarely the case. *The market trades in very wide ranges.* Since 1980, the market has had an average intrayear decline of 14.4 percent, *but still ended with a positive return 26 of the past 34 years!* (See Figure 1.8.) The market moves around a lot. Accept it, embrace it, learn to love it. If you can't do that, well then, at least get used to it!

You Can't Wait for Consumers to Feel Good

Bull markets are born on pessimism.

—John Templeton

You not only can't wait for things to "settle," you also can't use consumer confidence as an indicator. You might notice that during bear markets, commentators often talk a lot about "consumer confidence." They do this because the consumer drives a lot of the economy. If the consumer doesn't feel good, he likely won't spend money. If the consumer doesn't spend money then companies can't make money. And if companies don't make money, the markets likely won't recover. This is simply not true, primarily because the market isn't looking at

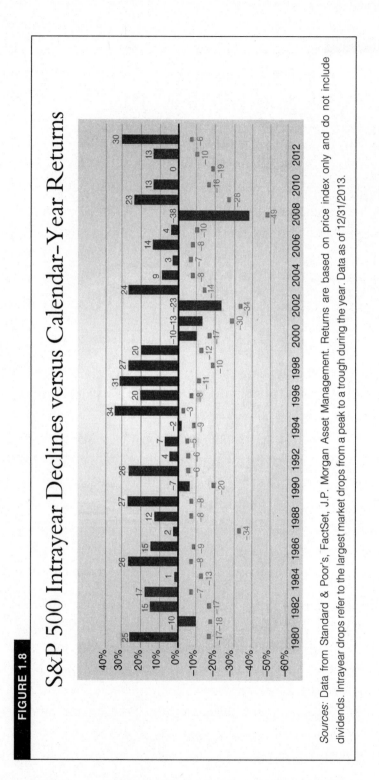

FIGURE 1.8

S&P 500 Intrayear Declines versus Calendar–Year Returns

Sources: Data from Standard & Poor's, FactSet, J.P. Morgan Asset Management. Returns are based on price index only and do not include dividends. Intrayear drops refer to the largest market drops from a peak to a trough during the year. Data as of 12/31/2013.

FIGURE 1.9

When the Consumer Gives Up

Consumer Confidence <60%	Next 12 Months (S&P 500)
1974	+37%
1980	+32%
1990	+30%
2008	+60%

today. The market is always looking at tomorrow. It cares less where the economy is today and more about where it is headed.

Bull markets tend to emerge when investors are *feeling the worst* about the future outlook. The University of Michigan regularly measures consumer confidence. Figure 1.9 shows how the stock market performed the 12 months following each time consumer confidence was less than 60 percent.*

Learning to Accept the Bear Markets

If you are 55 years old, you can expect to live through about seven or so more bear markets. Do you really want to freak out every time? Are you really going to navigate through each one? No, you're not, because you know better! There is one great thing that all bear markets have in common: 100 percent of the time, they give way to bull markets. Not 50 percent of the time, not 75 percent of the time, not 99 percent of the time. 100 percent of the time! Why do so many people mess with those

---

*My kids like to play the "opposite game" where you say the opposite of what you mean. Much of the market information that is intended to help investors, like the consumer confidence data, actually works the opposite of how commentators choose to reference it. We will see more of this later in the book when we look at Morningstar ratings.

odds? It makes no sense. But alas, for most, investing isn't about common sense. It's about emotions and the perception of control. More on that later!

Miscalculating the Risk of Market Timing

So, we have now established that market timing is dumb and doesn't work. You might be thinking though, "What's the big deal? So what if I miss some gains in exchange for safety?" This is the main objection to simply investing rather than market timing. The answer is quite simple. The risk of being out is far greater than the risk of being in.

Let's say you have a $25,000 bonus and you are deciding between investing and waiting for some arbitrary event to happen that will make you feel better about investing. If you invest all at once, one of three things will happen: The market will go up (hurray!), it will go sideways (very good—you get dividends!), or it will go down (still not a big deal because this is *temporary*). If it goes down, we know two things: First, we know you are going to collect dividends, which is better than what you get from cash, and second, we know the market will go back up. The downside is simply temporary—no big deal!

Now, if you wait in cash, the market can do the same three things: It can go up (you don't look so smart and lose a lot of money), it can go sideways (sorry, no dividends for you while you sit in cash), or it can go down (if you were too scared to go in today, are you really going to feel better in the middle of a correction? Be honest with yourself. We both know the answer is "no"!). Now, here's the rub. If you are in cash and the market goes up, you may have permanently lost the opportunity to capture the upside. For example, the Dow moved quickly from 10,000 to 16,000. Yes, it may go back down, but will it go back to 10,000? Maybe, but maybe not. If it doesn't go back down to that level, the investor sitting in cash will never be able to capture that return again. Being on the sideline often results in *permanently* missing the upside. On the other hand, if someone invests today, the worst thing that can happen is *temporarily* participating in the downside. Big difference.

But What If I Am Perfect?

Oh come on, really!? Well, there is always someone who thinks they can be perfect, that all the data and evidence don't apply to them, that they can find a way to make it happen. Let's take a look at just how much better off "that guy" will be if he is perfect. The Schwab Center for Financial Research evaluated five decisions available to an investor who has $2,000 in cash to invest once a year for 20 years (Riepe 2013):

1. Leave the money in cash.
2. Invest all at once each time.
3. Take the cash and dollar cost average into the market over the year, buying 1/12th each month.
4. Accidentally invest all of the money at the worst possible day every year (buying on the single day the market was the highest every single year).*
5. Fortuitously invest all of the money on the best possible day each year.† This is our Mr. Perfect. He always sits on the cash until the market is at the absolute lowest each year and then invests all the cash.

The results are nothing short of remarkable (see Figure 1.10). The perfect market timer ended up with $87,004, and right behind him in second place is the person who simply invested the money as soon as they received it (Riepe 2013).

Now, assuming you are in agreement that you are not going to invest all the cash you get on the single best day you can every single year for 20 years, investing the cash right away seems like a pretty good idea. Everything else provides various degrees of losing. Losing isn't fun, especially when it is so easy to win.

———————

*Wow, this person is unlucky! Or is he?
†I love this guy because he doesn't exist. He spends a lot of energy trying to convince you he is for real though.

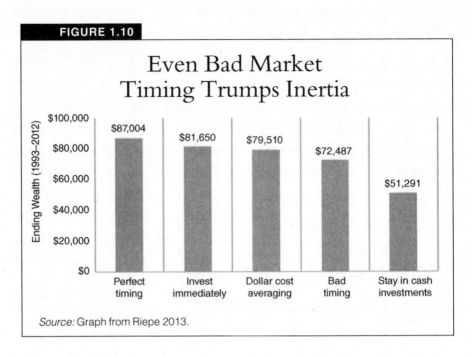

FIGURE 1.10

Even Bad Market Timing Trumps Inertia

Ending Wealth (1993–2012)

- Perfect timing: $87,004
- Invest immediately: $81,650
- Dollar cost averaging: $79,510
- Bad timing: $72,487
- Stay in cash investments: $51,291

Source: Graph from Riepe 2013.

Lump Sum Investing versus Dollar Cost Averaging

In the previous section we cover why, if you find yourself getting money each year, you should invest it all at once instead of over time. Surely, the advice is different if we are talking about a huge sum of money, right?

Surely dollar cost averaging instead of lump sum investing spreads out the risk? After all, it's a common recommendation given repeatedly by financial pundits and advisors to invest a lump sum over time. The answer is no, not really. It does however have legitimate psychological considerations that we will discuss in a minute.

First, what is a lump sum? A lump sum is when you get a boatload of money all at once. Examples are a large cash inheritance, proceeds from the sale of a business or real estate, a large gift (lucky you!), winning the lottery (super lucky you!), or a once-in-a-lifetime bonus. Lump sum investing refers to taking this lump sum and throwing it all into the market, all at once. Sounds crazy, right? Surely it's better to dollar cost average, which means investing in the market over time, such as investing 1/12th each month for 12 months.

Vanguard conducted a study comparing lump sum investing to dollar cost averaging (Shtekhman, Tasopoulos, and Wimmer 2012). They used an example of an investor who found himself with a million dollars in cash to invest and who ultimately wanted to be in a 60 percent stock and 40 percent bond portfolio. The researchers compared the impacts of lump sum investing to dollar cost averaging over 6, 12, 18, 24, 30, and 36 months. They also looked at the impact of this comparison in various markets, looking at the United States, United Kingdom, and Australia. They then examined the impact of both strategies over 10-year rolling periods, going all the way back to 1926. Finally, they repeated the study for a variety of portfolios, ranging from 100 percent bond all the way to 100 percent stock.

The conclusions are definitive. For an investor working their way to a 60/40 portfolio and holding it for 10 years, *67 percent of the time they ended up with more money by investing the lump sum as opposed to dollar cost averaging over 12 months*. This result persists across the three countries (see Figure 1.11).

Furthermore, lump sum investing's advantage was even more significant when compared to dollar cost averaging over longer periods of time (see Figure 1.12). For example, in the U.S. market, lump sum investing did better about 90 percent of the time when compared to dollar cost averaging over 36 months. At the end of the day, all the money is getting invested and is invested most of the time. The only period that is different is the period an investor is dollar cost averaging into the market.

So why does lump sum investing perform better than dollar cost averaging most of the time? The answer is simple: Bonds and stocks perform better than cash over time, and dollar cost averaging leaves some of the investor's money in cash during the entry period.

So you should always lump sum invest, right? Well, that depends on one important thing: you. Yes, the data is overwhelming that lump sum investing is better than dollar cost averaging most of the time. However, just because something is statistically in your favor doesn't mean it is right for you. One big factor to consider is the potential for regret.

FIGURE 1.11

Relative Historical Probability of Outperformance Using 12-Month DCA and a 60 Percent Stock/40 Percent Bond Portfolio

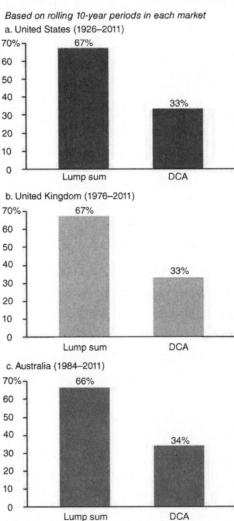

Based on rolling 10-year periods in each market

a. United States (1926–2011)

b. United Kingdom (1976–2011)

c. Australia (1984–2011)

Note: Each portfolio consists of a 60 percent allocation to the local equity market and a 40 percent allocation to the local bond market.

Source: Graph from Shtekhman, Tasopoulos, and Wimmer 2012, 3. Vanguard calculations based on benchmark data.

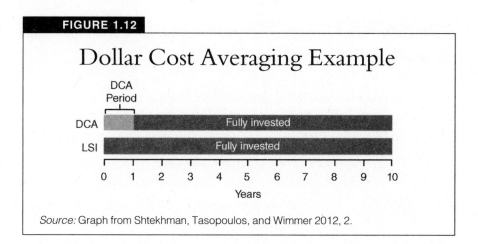

FIGURE 1.12

Dollar Cost Averaging Example

Source: Graph from Shtekhman, Tasopoulos, and Wimmer 2012, 2.

We are all familiar with regret. We may regret something we said or something we didn't say, a risk we did or didn't take, the one that got away, or some other decision we did or did not make.* Psychologists have extensively studied the impact of regret on decision making, and this research has expanded into the behavioral psychology of investing. One motivating factor for investors is fear of regret. This is the subconscious or fully conscious emotion that keeps us from selling a stock that is way up ("If I sell it, it may still go up and I'll regret it."), from selling a stock when it is down ("If I sell it, it may recover and I will regret it."), and from buying into the market when it is at an all-time high ("If I buy in, it may go down and I will regret it."). Fear of regret drives a lot of our personal decision making, and is a prevalent factor in investor decision making.

Let's go back to you and assume you have had a lifetime event leaving you with a pile of cash to invest, and you are facing the lump sum investing versus dollar cost averaging decision. If you are the type of person who plays the statistics, doesn't get emotional about market movements, and won't experience major regret if the market crashes the day after you invest, then lump sum investing is for you, and you will likely be better off for it.

---

*Right now, I am regretting eating a second helping of ice cream.

If you are the type of investor who will freak out if there is a market event (pick one—flash crash, tech bubble, 9/11, financial crisis, European debt crisis, etc.) the day after you invest, then spread it out a bit, and ease in over six months or so. Yes, you are most likely giving up some upside, but you will also be more likely to avoid regret and stick with the plan. In the end, the main point is to get invested—that's 90 percent of the game. The other 10 percent is getting invested as quickly as possible.

If you are going to dollar cost average, *commit to a calendar*, and invest as planned. For example, commit to investing 1/6th of the funds the first Monday of every month until you are fully invested. Otherwise, you may fall into the paralysis trap of seeing how you feel about the market each month, and sometimes hold back your investment. This is a loser's game.

The stats say to lump sum invest. The investor concerned with regret or willing to give up upside to avoid a short-term hit should consider dollar cost averaging. Both should have a plan to invest and stick to it.

Learning to Fly

I'm learning to fly, but I ain't got wings.

—Tom Petty

There comes a time when the baby birds need to leave the nest, take that jump, and learn to fly. Many investors have tried that before, only to land flat on their faces. Back in the nest, they struggle looking for a time to "take the jump" again.

If we look back though, there is no example in history of the stock market taking a dollar from anyone. Someone who had no idea what they were doing and simply bought the S&P 500 would have made huge profits over the past 10, 20, or 30 years. Truckloads of money have been lost, however, by investors making mistakes with their portfolio, or by using advisors who have made market timing or security selection mistakes. It is hard for most to believe that had an investor bought into the market at any time in history, they would have more money today than if they stayed in cash.

Let's take a look at the unluckiest investors:

The one who invested right before the 1987 crash: S&P 500 at 334

The one who invested right before the early 1990s recession: S&P 500 at 363

The one who invested the day before 9/11: S&P 500 at 1,096

The one who invested the day of the 2007 stock market high: S&P 500 at 1,526

All of these unlucky individuals did much better than the bird that stayed in the nest, waiting for the "right time" to take the jump. *As of April, 2014, the S&P 500 is at 1,878, but that does not include dividends, which averaged over 2 percent along the way and is the equivalent of approximately 300 more points since 2007.* Even the investors who went in at the worst possible times are far ahead of the "investor" sitting in cash, waiting for things to "settle down."

Many are scared off by the headlines that "the market is at an all-time high." Well, that is often true but it happens all the time. If that sounds too scary a time to enter the market, the odds are high you will never be comfortable.

The reply to this argument, of course, is that it is always better to enter after a market corrects or crashes. However, no one knows when that will happen, or more importantly, how high the market will go before it corrects. If the Dow goes from 15,000 to 16,000 then drops back to 15,000, what have you accomplished in this scenario by sitting in cash other than missing out on dividends? Also, I have yet to find the investor who is nervous at Dow 15,000 but feels super-fantastic about investing at Dow 13,000. If you are nervous when things are too good, you aren't going to feel better about investing when things don't look so hot.

For the disciplined investor, the time to invest is always today, and that is only because yesterday is no longer an option. You are ready to fly with the markets when you have knowledge to serve as your wings.

Avoiding Mistake #1—Market Timing

The evidence is overwhelming that market timing does not work. Academic research shows it, studies based on real-world managers substantiates it, the masses get it wrong, the media gets it wrong, economists get it wrong, investment managers get it wrong, and so does just about everybody else.

Market timing can be black and white, like going to cash and back to stocks. Often you are market timing and don't realize it ("I'll hold onto my bonus until the market settles."). Sometimes market timing is promoted by a money manager or financial advisor using coded language like "asset-class rotation," "downside protection," "tactical asset allocation," "style rotation," or "sector rotation." It's all market timing. Part of protecting yourself from this mistake is recognizing it.

Corrections are going to happen. Bear markets are going to happen. Bad things happen. No matter how nervous you get, no matter how bad things appear, the bear will give way to the bull. These corrections and bear markets will happen many times in your life, you can't predict them, and you will do more harm to your portfolio than good by trying to navigate your way through them by trading.

If an advisor tries to sell you any of these strategies, say "see ya later" and continue your search for another advisor. *If you are currently paying an advisor to do any of these things, know that you are willingly paying money to someone to increase the odds of your portfolio underperforming.* The research shows the pros can't do it. The odds are pretty darn high that you, your buddy, or your advisor can't do it either.

Active Trading

There are over 3,700 mutual funds that trade U.S. stocks and more than 7,000 U.S. hedge funds, many of which trade U.S. stocks. On top of that, there are actively managed exchange-traded funds (ETFs) that do the same, and thousands of separately managed account managers, brokers, and investment advisors also trading U.S. stocks. For good measure, let's throw in tens of millions of regular, everyday people all over the world who also trade U.S. stocks. That's a lot of people trading.

So how many U.S. stocks are all these people trading, you might ask? Maybe 100,000 exchange listed stocks? Nope. How about 25,000 exchange listed stocks? Nope. Under 4,000! That's right. There are less than 4,000 securities listed on the public exchanges (Krantz 2013)!

So, there are tens of thousands, if not hundreds of thousands of professionals plus tens of millions of other people trading these 4,000 or so stocks. This, of course, sounds silly.*

If we combine the 4,000 or so exchange listed stocks into one large portfolio, these stocks have a combined return called a *market return*. Common sense and basic arithmetic tells us that if people are trading within that portfolio, there must be winners and losers to the market return. Here's the rub though. Trading isn't free—there is always a cost. That means that there is a "house," you know, like Vegas. The house always wins. It gets paid no matter what. The house might be Merrill Lynch, UBS, Edward Jones, or one of hundreds of other brokers, but

---

* It sounds silly because it is silly. Pause for a moment and just imagine a visual of tens of millions of people all in the same place trading a few thousand things back and forth. It's preposterous really. That's the active trading that takes place in the stock market every day.

there is always, always a house. So by definition, there must be more losers than winners, and the winners must win enough to cover their transaction costs.

But wait, there's more. The winners must also pay taxes. This moves many of the winners over to the losers' column. Sorry, guys!

Hang on though, what about the winners who win enough to cover transaction costs and taxes? Well, there is no evidence that winners stay winners. In fact, there is a tremendous amount of evidence, as we shall see, that winners from the past are generally not winners in the future, and that eventually most winners become big-time losers. This is for a variety of reasons, including that some winners were just lucky, or they took excess risk to outperform and that same excess risk burns them later, or they make one of many of the mistakes outlined in this book.

Finally, one thing kills off almost all the winners: time. With time, the winners in the stock trading game tend to become losers.

Over 20-year periods, simply owning a basket of 500 of the largest stocks and never trading them outperformed over 80 percent of active traders (Ellis 2012). This is normal. There are lots of reasons for this. I will cover the reasons now with the goal that you will once and for all alleviate yourself of the temptation of playing the trading game—a game the pros can't win and that you likely can't win either. A game for suckers. You are not a sucker.

The History of Active Trading

History doesn't repeat itself, but it rhymes.

—Mark Twain

From January 1, 1928, to July 1, 1932, Alfred Cowles researched the ability of traders to beat the market (Cowles 1933). He reviewed 7,500 individual stock picks from 16 different financial services over a four-and-a-half-year period. He found that the professional stock picking resulted in underperformance of 1.43 percent. In other words, simply buying a bunch of stocks and doing nothing would have resulted in a much better outcome! Cowles went on to analyze the results of the very best stock pickers and concluded that the outcome was attributable to luck more than skill (more on this topic later).

From 1928 to 1931, Cowles also studied the stock picks of 20 insurance companies and found that they averaged an underperformance of 1.2 percent (Cowles 1933). Analyzing the winners, he found the best did not exhibit success due to skill, but rather by chance.

Nearly 100 years later, study after study shows that Cowles was onto something. Active management of stocks, regardless of how sophisticated, expensive, or complicated, results in underperformance over long periods of time, *almost all the time*.

Active Investment Managers Lose to Indexing

Active trading is dead. That is not something you hear on CNBC of late.

Active trading is being reinforced every day on cable channels, across almost every show, but especially propagated by Jim Cramer on his #1 CNBC rated show, *Mad Money*. In 2008, Jim Cramer bellowed that "investors should not follow Warren Buffett's lead this time around."

"Buy and Hold," Jim Cramer declared, "is dead."

The only problem with the perpetual hammering of this concept— the idea that active traders are making a killing while suckers are attempting to hold for the long term—is that *it is not true*.

In an effort to avoid being accused of cherry-picking comparisons, I will address, head on, the performance of the top players in each category:

1. Fisher Investments, run by the multibillionaire Ken Fisher, is one of the largest registered investment advisors serving high-net-worth clients.

2. Legg Mason Value is the only mutual fund to ever beat the S&P 500 15 years in a row.

3. Jim Cramer is the #1 market prognosticator (not based on performance, as we will discuss, but on television ratings).

The bottom line, as we will see, is that active traders routinely underperform the market, and the idea that smart people can trade stocks actively to improve performance is unfounded.

Fisher Investments

Giant insurer AIG ($57, AIG) is lower than it was one, three, five or even eight years ago—back when it sold for 40 times earnings. Now it is just 8 times earnings and 1.2 times annual revenue. But with an exceptionally strong presence in insurance and broader finance and slow but steady growth, it will enjoy a good run in the stock market in 2008.

—Ken Fisher providing one of his top-five
stock picks for 2008 in *Forbes**

Ken Fisher made an appearance in this book already because he is a market timer. He makes a second appearance here because he is also an active trader. His portfolio strategy is to attempt to beat the international index by active security selection while protecting his clients from downturns with market timing. According to Morningstar, this hasn't turned out so well with his mutual fund underperforming over the short run and the long run. His use of both active trading and market timing greatly increases the chances that his mutual fund, and his clients, will underperform.

Legg Mason Value

Hint: Money flows into most funds after good performance, and goes out when bad performance follows.

—John Bogle

You might ask why, out of the thousands of mutual funds, we must pick on Legg Mason Value. It is because you cannot find a better case study of the ultimate failure of active management. In November 2006, *Fortune* magazine made Legg Mason Value and its manager, Bill Miller, the subject of a feature story (Serwer 2006). Of the thousands of mutual funds that exist, Legg Mason Value was the only one that had beaten the S&P 500 for 15 years in a row. *Fortune* interviewed Bill, determined to show that it is possible to beat the market only if you have an edge. Otherwise, how can it possibly be done?

---

*AIG was saved from bankruptcy the same year by the government bailout.

(As an aside, here is how it is done: Take tens of thousands of professional money managers over 15 years, one of them will beat the market out of sheer probability. This is no different than someone betting "red" a dozen times in a row at a roulette table. The odds of success are miniscule that the person will hit red a dozen times in a row. However, if you have tens of thousands of people betting on red a dozen times in a row, someone will actually win each time—not out of skill, but out of the law of probability. The real surprise is not that Bill Miller beat the market so many years in a row, but that he was the only one to do it.)

In 2006, the year the *Fortune* story was published, Bill Miller underperformed the market. He underperformed the market again in 2007, and then again in 2008. In 2008 alone, Legg Mason Value was down a staggering 54 percent, or 17 percent worse than the market. Not only had the fund sustained devastating losses, but the losses were so severe that the fund now underperformed the market not only for 2008, but for the previous 5 years, 10 years, and since its inception. All it took was one year of poor stock selections to derail the performance of the past 15 years.

Wouldn't it have been nice if Bill Miller sent a letter with something like this in it to his clients:

> You are probably aware that Legg Mason Value Trust has outper-
> formed the S&P 500 Index for each of the last 15 calendar years. This
> may be the reason you decided to purchase the fund. If so, we are
> flattered, but believe you are setting yourself up for disappointment.
> Our so-called "streak" is a fortunate accident of the calendar. Over the
> past 15 years, the December to December time frame is the only one of
> the 12-month periods where our results have always outperformed the
> index. If your expectation is that we will outperform the market every
> year, you can expect to be disappointed.

Well, he did write that letter! Bill Miller knew the outperformance, year over year, was really a fluke of the calendar. Despite this, he couldn't have possibly known the dramatic fall to come.

The worst part is that the fund's collapse captured as many investors as possible. As is the case with any hot hand, money flowed to the mutual fund only after it showed it could beat the market many years in a row. Once the fund was awarded five stars by Morningstar, hyped in magazines and lauded for its manager's insight, investors poured in their money making it one of the largest funds in the country—*just in time to participate in the devastating losses.*

After the fall, more people pulled money out of the fund than at any time in its history.

There is little doubt that investors are now pouring what is left of their money into the hands of another market timer, who has had a great run recently.

Jim Cramer

Buy and hold is dead.

—Jim Cramer

No! No! No! Bear Stearns is fine! Do not take your money out!

—Jim Cramer

Jim Cramer is the ubiquitous host of CNBC's top-rated market timing show, *Mad Money*.

Jim started as a hedge fund manager in the 1980s. No one knows how he did as a money manager because he refuses to release audited performance figures. In 2006, Jonathan Clements, a reporter for the *Wall Street Journal*, asked him to share his performance figures, which Cramer refused.

Fortunately, Cramer has a show where he picks stocks, so we do not need to ask him how he is doing with stock picking. We can simply examine his record. Various financial researchers have documented that Cramer's picks consistently underperform the market. In August 2007, *Barron's* magazine published an article that measured his performance against the market using the 1,300 broadcasted *Mad Money* picks (Alpert 2007). Cramer's picks underperformed the NASDAQ by 2 percent, the S&P 500 by 4 percent, and the Dow Jones Industrial Average by 10 percent for the period of July 28, 2005, to August 17, 2007. Cramer assailed these studies saying it is hard to track his performance from his on-air comments.

He claimed the definitive way to track his performance was to look at his picks on TheStreet.com. Cramer endorsed the site, saying it is "exactly what I say, when I said it, and how I feel about each stock now."

In February 2009, *Barron's* responded to Cramer's challenge by reviewing the performance of his stock picks listed on the website (Alpert 2009). Their results showed Cramer's Buy recommendations performed 7 *percent worse than the market* from May to December of 2013. If you compare both his Buy and Sell recommendations to the market, instead of just his Buy recommendations, he underperforms the market by 5 percent. Yet again, Cramer's producers disputed *Barron's* study, saying TheStreet.com accidentally misinterpreted four of Cramer's Buy recommendations. On one recommendation, they said Cramer was being sarcastic and was not serious about the Buy. *Barron's* reran the performance figures without the four disputed points, and according to *Barron's*, the "performance was precisely as bad without them" (Alpert 2009).

Jim Cramer has yelled some recommendations about which he has been profoundly wrong. He screamed "No! No! No! Bear Stearns is fine! Do not take your money out!" the same week the stock was destroyed and folded into JP Morgan (Alpert 2009). He has obviously yelled many things that turned out to be right (you are more likely to find those in the commercials). The bottom line is that Jim Cramer has lost to the market over the short run and over the long run, whether you count his Buys, his Buys and Sells, the TV picks, or the website version. The fact is he has simply underperformed the market, consistently.

In October 2008, Jeremy Siegel, considered one of the greatest market statisticians, was asked by *Fortune* if he agreed with Jim Cramer that buy and hold was dead (O'Keefe 2008). *Fortune* told Siegel that CNBC's Jim Cramer declared, "You haven't made any money in ten years, so buy–and–hold must come into question" (O'Keefe 2008). Siegel responded: "I'm overwhelmed by the emptiness of that idea. The history of the market is precisely the opposite" (O'Keefe 2008).

So, when you hear the prognosticators on CNBC or Fox Business News yell about their trades, ask yourself why they do not track their results on the air. It is because they do not want you to know their true performance relative to the market. If you hear advisors on TV or your local radio claim that they hold the keys to stock picking success, know this:

They are selling a lie.

Newsletters Lose to Indexing

Many investment newsletters offer market timing advice. As we discussed in Chapter 1, those letters don't do so well. The newsletters that provide stock picks don't perform so well either. Study after study shows that most newsletters don't even survive for 10 years. Those that do survive, as a group, lose to the market, and those that do beat the market do not continue to beat the market (Graham and Campbell 1994). Particularly entertaining is a point Mark Hulbert made about going "all in" based on past performance. Looking at 1986 to 2006, Hulbert found that if you took $1,000,000 in 1985 and invested it per the recommendation of the previous year's top-rated newsletter, and repeated this strategy for all 16 years, you would have amassed $365, or an average annual loss of 31.4 percent (Young 2007)! So, just because a newsletter gets its stock picks more right than all the others in any given year doesn't mean that you should put more money into their recommendations the next year!

Active Mutual Funds Lose to Indexing

On average, it's a simple fact that passive indexing always has and always will outperform active fund management—it's as certain as night follows day in this uncertain business.

—John Bogle

As we start, let's clear the air a bit. There is a raging debate in the investment world as to whether passive management (owning a market index) beats active management (trading stocks in any given market). For example, a U.S. large cap mutual fund manager's performance is often compared to the S&P 500 Index, a well-known U.S. large cap index. Likewise, an international fund manager may be compared to the MSCI EAFE Index. For every major market, there is an index (a large sampling of stocks) for a manager's performance to be judged against. The passive versus active debate is a heated one, but an illogical one. *It is a fact, not an opinion, that passive indexed investing, on the whole, handily beats active trading.* Let me repeat: This is a *fact*. Now, some would like to debate whether *some* active managers can beat the index. We will come to that later. For now, let's cover the evidence.

The objective of an actively managed fund is to outperform its benchmark, whether it is the S&P 500 or any other index. Thanks to extensive databases tracking performance, many researchers have studied this topic. The conclusion, over and over again, is that in any given 12-month period, about 60 percent of mutual fund managers under-perform (Ellis 2012). Over 10 years, the percentage of managers under-performing tops 70 percent (Ellis 2012). Over 20 years, the percentage of managers underperforming is about 80 percent (Ellis 2012). Again, these are facts, not opinions (see Figure 2.1).

FIGURE 2.1

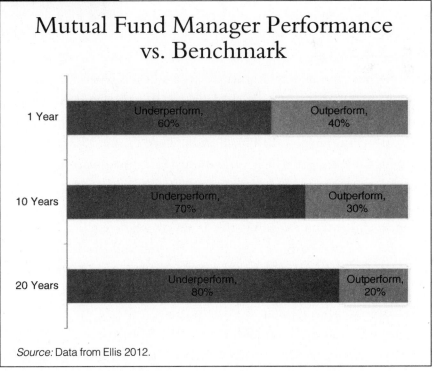

Mutual Fund Manager Performance vs. Benchmark

1 Year	Underperform, 60%	Outperform, 40%
10 Years	Underperform, 70%	Outperform, 30%
20 Years	Underperform, 80%	Outperform, 20%

Source: Data from Ellis 2012.

Survivor Bias (a.k.a. Mutual Funds Perform Even Worse Than the Data Suggests)

. . . if you look at the aggregate results of the mutual-fund industry on an after-fee, after-tax basis and adjust it for survivorship bias, the probability that you are going to end up with market-beating returns is de minimus . . . the 10-year after-tax shortfall for mutual funds is 4.5 percent per year relative to what you would have gotten if you had put your money in an index fund.

—David Swenson, Chief Investment Officer at Yale University, in an interview with the *Wall Street Journal*'s Tom Lauricella in 2005

Mutual funds that underperform persistently are often closed. I don't mean closed to new investors, I mean closed down, shut down, "dead." In a study covering the impact of "survivorship bias" on mutual fund statistics, researchers examined 2,364 mutual funds that shut down from January 1996 through December 2011 (Schlanger and Philips 2013). They found, unsurprisingly, that the main reason for the closure of the mutual funds was underperformance. The researchers then looked at the surviving funds over the same time period and found that in nearly every category, including every major U.S. market, actively managed funds underperformed the index. Once the funds that closed were added back into the mix, the underperformance became even worse.

So what? Well, these funds are eliminated from databases that investors use to make decisions. Survivor bias makes it appear as if these funds, often the worst performing of the bunch, didn't even exist at all! For example, Morningstar Principia, which tracks mutual fund performance, eliminates closed funds from its screens. In one comprehensive study, researchers added back all the closed funds from 1995 to 2004 and found that in 41 of 42 Morningstar fund categories, the result was a difference of 1.6 percent per year over the entire 10-year period (Barrett and Brodeski 2006). In other words, the actual performance of active mutual funds, which already as a group underperformed their index benchmarks, was actually 1.6 percent per year worse than the data suggests!

In another study, researchers examined 1,540 actively managed U.S. mutual funds from 1998 to 2012 (Wimmer, Chhabra, and Wallick 2013).

They found that of those funds, only 55 percent survived, and the percentage that survived and outperformed was just 18 percent (see Figure 2.2).

The takeaway is straightforward: The data makes it clear that mutual funds underperform their respective benchmark indexes, and the data doesn't even accurately represent the degree of underperformance.*

What About the Winners, Huh? What About the Winners?!

Don't look for the needle in the haystack. Just buy the haystack!

—John Bogle

In any given year, there are winners. While the majority of mutual funds tend to lose to the index, some beat it. The issue is that they tend to not outperform over and over, and there is absolutely no indication that the performance persists. In fact, we know that over time, performance almost always gives way to underperformance.

One great example of this is looking at the 50 hottest-selling mutual funds in 2000. They lost an average of 42 percent over the next five years. Only two of the funds made money over the five-year period, up 1.5 and 2.3 percent, respectively. The losses would have been less severe had you put your money in the 50 largest mutual funds. They lost 15 percent over the same time period. Over the same time period, the S&P 500 Index was up just over 1 percent. The 50 funds that saw

---

*It is dumbfounding that funds that closed aren't included. Imagine that you were in a race against 10 people and you came in first but half the people were so out of shape they couldn't finish the race. We would say you beat nine people, not four. When a team wins the World Series, we don't say they finished in first out of two teams, we include all the teams that didn't survive to make it to the World Series. The ones that didn't survive need to be included. Everyone seems to understand this concept except for money managers.

FIGURE 2.2

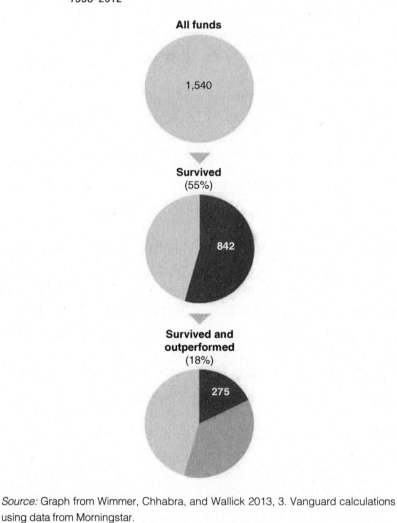

A Small Portion of Active Funds Survived *and* Outperformed Over 15 Years

The fate of 1,540 actively managed U.S. equity funds, 1998–2012

All funds

1,540

Survived
(55%)

842

Survived and outperformed
(18%)

275

Source: Graph from Wimmer, Chhabra, and Wallick 2013, 3. Vanguard calculations using data from Morningstar.

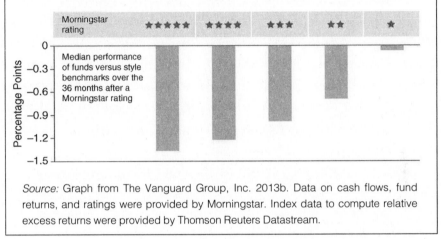

Source: Graph from The Vanguard Group, Inc. 2013b. Data on cash flows, fund returns, and ratings were provided by Morningstar. Index data to compute relative excess returns were provided by Thomson Reuters Datastream.

the most redemptions in the 12 months ending March 2000 had gained an average 21.4 percent* (Waggoner 2005).

Let's take a more comprehensive look. Morningstar uses star ratings to evaluate mutual funds. If a fund scores in the top 10 percent of its category, it receives five stars; in the next 22.5 percent, four stars; in the middle 35 percent, three stars; in the next 22.5 percent, two stars; and in the bottom 10 percent, one star. Well, that makes it pretty easy. If a mutual fund has five stars, we should just buy it, right? Not so fast.

Analyzing data from June 1993 through December 2012, Vanguard plotted the performance of the mutual funds for the 36 months after their star rating (The Vanguard Group, Inc. 2013b). (See Figure 2.3.) *The mutual funds that received five stars actually performed the worst and those with one star performed the best.* The star chart actually works in the reverse way

---

*It's amazing how little patience investors have. They leave funds right before they recover and go into funds right before they collapse. Over and over and over again.

intended. Using this data, an investor is far more likely to outperform going forward by choosing a one-star-rated mutual fund!

If there are thousands of professional managers, surely some will outperform, if only because it is statistically normal for some to do so. Sometimes they outperform because they take excess risks, in which case those risks often come back to haunt them. The overall lesson, though, is that the short-term outperformance is usually due to luck or because a manager is taking excess risks. The luck eventually runs out, or the risks eventually play out. There is a reason investments have the disclaimer: "*Past performance is not an indicator of future results.*" That reason is because it is not indicative *at all* of future results!

The typical investor, unfortunately, doesn't understand any of this. And how could they when the entire industry, investment managers, and the media keep promoting the concept that recent outperformance means something. The consequences for the typical investor though are quite severe. Remember how the four- and five-star-rated funds have actually performed the worst going forward? *Well, from 2000 to 2010, four- and five-star-rated funds took in 72 percent of all new assets placed into mutual funds* (Willoughby 2010). The pattern continues and investors will likely continue to take shortcuts to evaluate investments that cause far more harm than good.

Hedge Funds Lose to Indexing

I want to pay more in fees, pay more in taxes, give up access to my investment, not know exactly what is going on with my money, and get below-average returns.
                                                              —Said no one, ever.

In 2008, Warren Buffett made a 10-year bet with Ted Seides, a partner at the hedge fund company, Protégé. Warren and Ted bet a million dollars, to be paid to the other's favorite charity, with Warren claiming that hedge funds could not beat the market, and Ted claiming that they most certainly can. Warren was so confident that he even let Ted choose the hedge funds rather than simply comparing the performance of the overall stock market to the overall hedge fund market. In other words, this is a bet between owning the S&P 500, a basket of non-traded stocks, and five funds of hedge funds, the cream of the crop, hand selected by Seides. Protégé's website claims that hedge funds beat the market while taking less risk.* Buffett claims that is all hooey, and says hedge funds can't come close to justifying their fees.

I am a believer in using multiple asset classes including stocks, bonds, real estate, commodities, and some publicly traded alternatives. However, there should be no place in a portfolio for hedge funds. There are lots of reasons, but the main one is simple: *Investing in hedge funds is a great way to increase the odds of <u>underperformance</u>*. This goes against most of what you will hear about these investment vehicles, so let's look at the facts.

Hedge funds are private investment funds available to eligible investors who engage in a wide range of activities. Some hedge funds are "event driven," meaning they try to gain an edge on the markets based on major events such as wars, oil shortages, economic events, and so on. Some are long/short funds, meaning they bet on some stocks going up and others going down. Some use derivatives and options and many use leverage (borrow money to invest). This all just scratches the surface. The main objective of many of these funds is to deliver the stock market return or an even better return, with less volatility.

I never use hedge funds because I am well aware of what drives future performance, and hedge funds start out with a great disadvantage *in every major category*: taxes, fees, risk management, transparency, and liquidity.

First, for high-net-worth individuals, the top indicator of future performance, after asset allocation, is taxes. You should always be actively working to reduce taxes. Hedge funds do the opposite. With active trading, nearly all hedge fund managers deliver a much larger tax hit than owning an index. Strike one.

Second, most hedge funds have ridiculously high fee schedules, with the typical fee being an annual management fee of 1.5 to 2 percent whether the portfolio is up or down, plus 20 percent of the profits (if

---

*I hope you still have your BS meter on. These hedge fund guys take the cake by taking total garbage, making it look like candy, and selling the heck out of it.

there are profits).* Given that fees are a major indicator of future performance, let's call this strike two.

Third, while we are discussing how hedge fund managers get paid, it is interesting to note that the manager has a great incentive to take huge risks with your money. If the manager gets paid 2 percent no matter what happens, plus a huge percentage of the profits, well, why not go for it? It is not uncommon for a hedge fund to go up 30 percent, make the manager a centimillionaire or billionaire, and then blow up a year later, at no negative consequence to the manager. This just happened in 2012 when the top manager from the previous year saw his fund lose nearly half its value with abysmal performance. The consequence to the manager who made several billion the year before was simply a little embarrassment. He will likely get over it. I prefer to understand the risks in a given portfolio and control them. Strike three.

As if that isn't enough, hedge funds do not regularly disclose what they own or what their strategy even is at any given time. Therefore, the investor often has no idea what they own or the risks they are exposed to at any given period. With most hedge funds, you simply wait for the statement to see what happened. I am a big believer in transparency. At any given time, you should know what you own and how your investments are doing, and retain the flexibility to take appropriate action.†

Finally, hedge funds lack liquidity. Hedge fund investors usually need to wait for "windows" to open so they can redeem their funds. Indexes provide liquidity, giving you the ability to exit positions at any given time.

Now, why in the world would anyone invest in hedge funds when they know they will pay more taxes, pay fees 100 to 500 percent+ higher, take less control over their risk, lose transparency, and lose the ability to exit the investment whenever they wish? Well, the answer is quite simple: performance.

---

* This is a big if. The failure rate of hedge funds is very high. More on that later.
† Hedge funds as an investment already struck out, so no need to keep counting strikes.

Only one problem: The hedge fund performance myth isn't really a myth. It's a lie.

Hedge funds aren't scarce and they aren't special. It may surprise you to know there are more than 10,000 hedge funds!

In 2012, Goldman Sachs, analyzing hedge funds using public filings, found the S&P 500 returned *more than double* the average hedge fund. According to the *Wall Street Journal, 2013 marked the fifth year in a row that hedge funds lagged the stock market index.* Simply investing in a 60/40 portfolio (60 percent stocks and 40 percent bonds) would have resulted in performing better than hedge funds seven of the last eight years and each of the last six years.

Keep in mind too that most hedge funds perform so poorly, they don't even survive. A recent study examined all 6,169 unique hedge funds (eliminating those not in U.S. currency and those that are "funds of funds") from 1995 through 2009 (Chen 2013). Of these 6,169 that were around in 1995, only 2,252 were still around at the end of the study in 2009. The other 3,917 were dead. That means if you invested in a hedge fund in 1995, the odds it even did well enough to survive were just 37 percent. Not good.

You may be thinking, "What about the best hedge funds?" The best hedge funds are the ones that often have the most spectacular downfalls. Long-Term Capital Management, run by Nobel Prize winners and considered the greatest hedge fund of its time, collapsed overnight and nearly took the markets down with it in 1998. Warren Buffett, who has repeatedly stated he finds hedge funds to be ridiculous invest-ments, said of the Long-Term Capital Management fiasco: "They probably have as high an average IQ of any sixteen people working together in one business in the country . . . just an incredible amount of intellect in that group. Now you combine that with the fact that those sixteen had extensive experience in the field they were operating in . . . in aggregate, the sixteen probably had 350 to 400 years of experience doing exactly what they were doing. And then you throw in the third factor: that most of them had virtually all of their substantial net worth's in the business. . . . And essentially they went broke . . . that to me is fascinating."

Madoff's hedge fund emerged as the new gold standard. A hard lesson regarding transparency was learned by many. The most recent hedge fund star, John Paulson, had called the mortgage crisis and used his hedge fund to bet correctly. His investors made huge returns and he made billions, all in one year. Unfortunately for his investors, he lost 52 percent in 2011, when the market was up (Vardi 2012).

Hedge funds earned basically nothing during a full market cycle. From 2008 to the present we saw a drop, periods of stagnation, and a huge gain. This is the type of market in which hedge funds are supposed to perform the best. Where are the better returns with less risk? They simply don't exist. Instead, hedge funds have proven, once again, that they are really handmade for suckers.

Hedge fund defenders* will say that while the purpose of hedge funds used to be to outperform the market, now the purpose is simply to reduce portfolio volatility. However, a study covering the period of 2002 through 2013 looked at the performance of hedge funds that largely attempt to reduce volatility and compared the results to owning a simple 60 percent stock index, 40 percent bond index portfolio. The results are the simple indexed portfolio not only outperformed the hedge funds, *it did so with less volatility* (Housel 2014).

Now, back to the bet between Warren Buffett and Ted Seides. At just past the halfway mark through the 10-year bet, Warren's S&P 500 index is up nearly 43.8 percent and Ted's hedge funds are up 12.5 percent.

Yes, hedge funds will make someone rich. Just likely not you.†

Endowments—Misperception of Performance

We have all heard about endowments performing so well using alternative investments in their portfolio. How does that square with all the evidence that active investments like hedge funds don't work out so well?

---

* Who are usually people running them or selling them.
† But the hedge fund managers will continue to laugh all the way to the bank or their yachts. How foolish they must think we all are. And we have given them plenty of reason to think that.

To understand the difference, we need to understand the world of endowments.

Only 9 percent of endowments manage $1 billion or more (Wallick, Wimmer, and Schlanger 2012). We hear about these endowments all the time in the media—Yale, Harvard, and so on. A study examining publicity around endowments found that an investor was 10 times more likely to hear or read a story about one of the 10 largest endowments than one about the other 823 endowments. These 10 largest endowments, as a group, actually have done better than the market over the last 25 years by a few percentage points. However, it is important to understand how they are doing it. They have huge teams of investors who are investing directly into many investments. For example, rather than buying into a hedge fund investing in timber land, the endowment just buys the timber land directly. In fact, they do this 96 percent of the time (Wallick, Wimmer, and Schlanger 2012). Assuming you aren't going to buy a mine in Tanzania or 10,000 acres of land in Peru, this just isn't an option for you.

The other 91 percent of endowments haven't had much luck using hedge funds, private equity funds, active managers, and the like. These 91 percent of endowments see the large endowments having success investing in alternative investments so they go buy them too. What they are missing is that the large endowments are having success because they buy *directly* and have a purchasing power advantage. Trying to replicate the success, the other 91 percent of endowments, as a group, have increased their allocation to expensive alternative investments with small endowments now at 17 percent alternatives and medium endowments at 37 percent alternatives (Wallick, Wimmer, and Schlanger 2012). The results have not worked out well for them. Over the 10 years ending June 30, 2011, the average endowment underperformed a simple 60 percent stock/40 percent bond index combination (Wallick, Wimmer, and Schlanger 2012). The lesson here is unless you are a multibillionaire, forget about replicating the 10 largest endowments. They are basically running a business by buying investments directly. Instead, outperform all the other endowments by avoiding indirect, expensive, underperforming investments like hedge funds.*

Venture Capital (Sounds Sexy but Usually a Dog)

We have met the enemy and he is us.

—Pogo†

Private equity investments are about as sexy as you can get, and the subset of venture capital—which is an investment in startups—is the coolest subset of the bunch. Many investors and even institutions have the misperception that venture capital funds produce outsized returns. Many of America's greatest companies were born from venture capital funds, including Google and Apple. The Kauffman Foundation, with its $2 billion fund, is one of the largest endowments in the country. In 2012, they released a groundbreaking paper on their experience with venture capital funds, aptly titled: "We Have Met the Enemy . . . And He Is Us." I love the subtitle too: "Lessons from Twenty Years of the Kauffman

---

*You might be thinking, "Come on. These endowments must be run by really smart people. Surely, they know all of this and wouldn't make these mistakes." Unfortunately, that's not the case. The financial services industry perpetuates misinformation and continually judges performance incorrectly. In fact, it is common industry practice for endowments to hire consultants who review performance of hedge funds and mutual funds and then recommend the ones that performed the best over the last three or five years. This makes no sense and contributes to their perpetual underperformance.

†Pogo is not a philosopher or money manager. He is the main character of a comic strip from the 1940s that stayed popular through the early 1980s. For readers under 30, a comic strip is a sequence of drawings arranged in boxes to display humor, typically printed in a newspaper. (For those under 20, a newspaper is a printed publication consisting of folded sheets containing news, articles, editorial, advertisements, and sometimes comic strips.)

Foundation's Investments in Venture Capital Funds and the Triumph of Hope over Experience."

The Kauffman Foundation analyzed their personal experience with 100 venture capital funds over 25 years. Among their findings were the majority of venture capital funds underperformed the publicly available small cap index, only 4 of 30 venture capital funds with over $400 million in committed capital outperformed the small cap index, and the average venture capital fund ". . . fails to return the capital invested after fees." This is especially troubling since while the companies that venture capital funds invest in are small, they are much, much smaller than small cap companies that comprise the publicly available index. This means venture capital funds are far riskier. In other words, not only did venture capital funds underperform, they did so with far more risk as well as with higher fees (2 percent plus 20 percent of profits is the norm), less liquidity (investments often locked up for as much as a decade or more), and less transparency (what do we really know about what is going on in a private startup company anyway?).

The conclusion of the report is straightforward: Investors are likely better off investing in a small cap index fund than a venture capital fund. The researchers wrote, ". . . investors like us succumb time and again to narrative fallacies, a well-studied behavioral finance bias" (Mulcahy, Weeks, and Bradley 2012, p. 3). In other words, investments in venture capital funds are based largely on a story that looks backward to explain events as well as on the allure of the promised higher returns.

Assuming you still have an interest in investing in venture capital, and are confident the fund you invest in will do what the Kauffman Foundation's venture capital funds failed to do, note that unlike the Kauffman Foundation, which is a charity, you will owe taxes on any gains you receive. So if you find yourself overcoming the investment return odds, the tax gods will set you back. For most investors interested in investing in an asset class that has a high probability of outperforming large company stocks over 10 years or more, small cap index investing, not venture capital, is the answer.

The Taxman Commeth
(a.k.a. Dear Goodness, It Gets Worse)

Should five percent appear too small, be thankful I don't take it all, 'cause I'm the taxman, yeah I'm the taxman.

—"The Taxman" from the Beatles Album, *Revolver*

When a mutual fund, hedge fund, or index fund publishes its returns, it is always showing you *pre-tax* returns. Keep in mind that the entire point of an actively managed fund is to outperform a specific benchmark or index; otherwise there is no point in using the manager. Well, to beat the index, the active manager usually trades securities. The fund doesn't pay the taxes that result from the trading; you do! The average mutual fund loses a full percent, *every year*, to taxes (The Vanguard Group, Inc. 2013a). So, if the mutual fund performance shows a return of 6 percent, it's really 5 percent after you pay the tax man. The results are even worse for hedge fund managers who are, as a group, even more active traders. Index funds have tax consequences too as stocks are added to or dropped off the index, but because there are no active traders, the consequences are far less.

At the end of the day, it doesn't matter what you earn. What matters is what you earn *after taxes*. Keep in mind that indexes beat active managers even before taxes are taken into consideration. Taxes just widen the performance gap even further.

Portfolio Activity Hurts Performance

My favorite holding period is forever.

—Warren Buffett

We know that mutual funds, hedge funds, and investment managers who trade stocks underperform the index as a group. Research not only shows that active trading underperforms, but that the more active the manager is, the more likely they are to underperform.

Brigham Young University professor Craig Israelsen examined the returns of U.S. stock, U.S. bond, and International Stock mutual fund managers over 3-, 5-, and 10-year periods (Israelsen 2010). He divided the funds into four groups based on how actively they trade.

In every single case, and over every single time period, the funds with the most activity underperformed the funds with the least activity. *In other words, the more active and involved the manager, the worse the funds performed!* Over 10 years, the low turnover U.S. managers outperformed the high turnover managers by 2.2 percent *per year*, with the outperformance of low turnover International managers at 1.6 percent per year and low turnover bond managers at .2 percent per year.

The less the manager traded, the better the investors did. If you want to trade way less, skip the mutual funds, skip the hedge funds, skip the investment managers who actively trade, and focus the core of your portfolio on indexes.

But Doesn't Active Management Work in a Down Market?

Bear markets happen all the time, and when they happen, managers flood TV, radio, and letters saying that active management is needed more than ever. This helps keep a popular myth alive: The myth that active managers can at least outperform when the market is down. This is simply not true. In the seven bear markets since 1973, active managers outperformed just three times (Philips, Kinniry, and Schlanger 2013). They didn't make up for it when things turned around either, underperforming in six of the last eight bull markets (Philips, Kinniry, and Schlanger 2013). Overall, active managers lose in up markets, sideways markets, and down markets; they just underperform by a smaller percentage in a down market.

When we look at two of the worst modern-day bear markets, from 2000 to 2002 and the 2008 crisis, the results are the same. In every major category, the index beat the active manager (see Figure 2.4).

Why Indexes Win

Passive investing beats active investing for many reasons. First, active trading dilutes returns due to transaction costs. Second, active

FIGURE 2.4

Myth Dispelled

Percent of Active Funds Outperformed by Benchmarks in Bear Markets		
Fund Category	**2008**	**2000 to 2002**
All Large-Cap Funds	54.3	53.5
All Mid-Cap Funds	74.7	77.3
All Small-Cap Funds	83.8	71.6

management costs substantially more. Third, active management generates more taxes. Fourth, the typical active manager sits on more cash than an index fund, and this cash drag hurts returns over time. Fifth, active managers fall prey to the same behavioral mistakes that everyday investors make (more on this later).

There is another big reason why indexes outperform. It's because of the variance of returns among stocks. Most people think an index contains a basket of stocks, half of which outperform the market and half of which underperform the market. This is just not how it works. Inside an index, nearly two-thirds of stocks underperform the index itself, while about one-third outperform. How can this be? It's because when a stock goes down, the worst thing that can happen is a loss of 100 percent (see Lehman Brothers, Enron, MF Global, and so on). However, when a stock takes off, the sky is the limit and the return can go up thousands of percentage points (see Apple, Google, Microsoft, and so on). A big winner can offset many losers. If you have a basketball team with 10 players and they score 100 points, we don't assume half scored more than 10 and half scored less than 10. In reality, one or two players can score the majority of the points. It's the same with the market. By casting a wide net with the index, you are more likely to catch the next high flyer.

But Indexing Results in Average Returns

Indexing not only does not result in average returns, it all but guarantees that over time, you will have above average returns. The only question is how above average the returns will be. Most of the time, the returns are far above average. Over the 20 years ending January 1, 2014, indexes in various categories outperformed 71 to 85 percent of actively managed funds (The Vanguard Group, Inc. 2013b). Does that sound average to you? Indexing will put you in the winner's circle if you let it.*

S&P 500, Here I Come!

Don't put all your eggs in one basket.

—English proverb

Well, then. Let's toss all our money in the S&P 500 and move on with life! Not so fast. Investing doesn't need to be overly complicated, but it's not that easy. Let's look at a recent decade to see why asset allocation matters.

Much has been made about the negative return of the market from 2000 through 2010.

It is enlightening to put one of the worst decades in stock market history into proper context. First, commentators often like to refer to this decade as the "Lost Decade," and cite it as proof that owning the market doesn't work. In fact, it is a testament to quite the opposite conclusion. First, it is important to note that when people say "the market" lost money over that decade, they are referring to the S&P 500 Index. In fact, this index represents just part of the market: The S&P 500 is exclusively U.S. stocks and exclusively large companies.

A graph tells the story quite nicely (see Figure 2.5).

As with all previous bear markets, the well-allocated investor weathered the storm quite nicely. By properly allocating the portfolio, the investor not only took on less risk, but also earned better returns. Since it is impossible to identify which asset class will outperform on a

---

*And you need to let it!

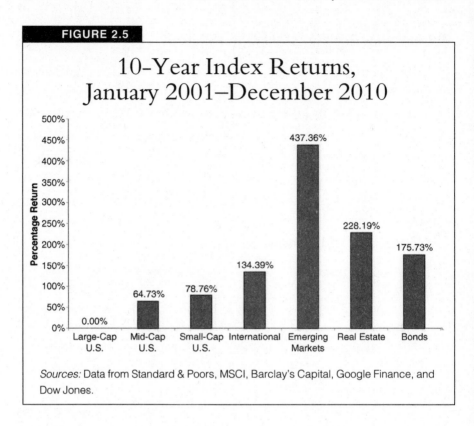

FIGURE 2.5

10-Year Index Returns, January 2001–December 2010

Sources: Data from Standard & Poors, MSCI, Barclay's Capital, Google Finance, and Dow Jones.

year-by-year basis, the prudent investor invests for the long run and *is never dependent on the short-term performance of one market.*

The next time someone talks to you about the "Lost Decade" as a reason to market time or actively trade stocks, remind them that a simple asset allocation made the decade quite profitable for a sensible investor. The other markets—energy, real estate, emerging markets, international, and mid-cap and small-cap U.S. markets—were up.

Also, charts like the one used here actually understate how well the investor actually performed. The S&P 500, in fact, was actually up a few percentage points when dividends are included, and since the investor received them, it seems sensible to count them. All in all, while owning just the S&P 500 would have been extremely unpleasant, someone who simply allocated their portfolio across various asset classes and ignored the assault of bear markets throughout the decade did quite well, even during one of the worst periods in all history to be an investor.

Avoiding Mistake #2—Active Trading

We know that simple math tells us the majority of active managers—whether mutual fund managers, hedge fund managers, brokers, investment managers, or you—must underperform. We also know that active management costs more than owning an index. Let's add on that active managers create more taxes than passive managers. Finally, we know when we do find an active manager who outperforms, there is no evidence that suggests the outperformance will continue. In fact, there is extensive evidence suggesting quite the opposite.

So, we know with certainty we will pay more in fees. We know with certainty we will pay more in taxes. We know there is a high probability of underperformance even before fees and taxes. This seems pretty clear. Maybe active management isn't the way to go.

With all of this knowledge, why do so many of us actively trade, hire fund managers who trade, or hire investment managers who trade? Because we all want to believe it can be done. We are Americans, for goodness sakes! Someone can always outperform, there is always a way to beat the street or to game the system. Well, if you hand your money to an active manager, someone is getting gamed all right. It's you.

Misunderstanding Performance and Financial Information

There are many myths that persist in the investment management field, a few because of investors' biases, some because they make for cute stories in the media, and many because professionals encourage and perpetuate them. In this chapter, we will take a look at some of the most common misperceptions.

Misunderstanding #1—Judging Performance in a Vacuum

A friend shared with me the performance of one of the money managers being offered to them. Basically, the manager was saying, "Hey, look at how awesome this portfolio has performed; put your money in this!" While this may literally be the single worst way to make a decision regarding investments, the reality is that this is how most Americans choose their portfolio, whether it is anything from a separately managed account to a mutual fund.

So what is the problem with this strategy? It is a function of misunderstanding "reference sets" and it results in poor decision making.

Reference sets can best be explained this way: Assume you have a room full of 12,000 people and tell them to flip a coin. If you repeat this about 13 times, someone will likely have flipped heads every time. We should not marvel at the brilliance of such a person. Rather, we should expect this outcome.

If we visit a Las Vegas casino and find someone winning at roulette, we don't hand them all our money. Rather, we know this is one gambler in a reference set full of gamblers and that most of them are losing. In his book, *The Black Swan*, Nassim Taleb calls this the reference point argument, which he describes as not computing odds from the vantage point of a winning gambler, but from that of all the gamblers who started at the same time (Taleb 2007). We know that in fact some people give their money to the "hot hand" gambler to bet for them. These people are shortsighted and are exhibiting the exact same behavior as an investor giving all their money to the latest fund manager on a winning streak.

This is essentially how most money managers market their success stories. For example, it is not uncommon for a money manager to manage 6 to 10 portfolios or funds. It is not surprising that one or two of these outperform their benchmark. Slick glossies and PowerPoint presentations are then made to tout the performance, completely ignoring the majority of portfolios or funds that did not meet or beat their benchmark. Investors buy in, the fund eventually underperforms, the manager then touts another portfolio, the investor moves to the next hot hand, and so on.

The same strategy is used by mutual fund companies. As with all decades, from 2000 to 2010, most large company mutual fund managers underperformed the S&P 500. That is quite a spectacular feat when you consider the S&P 500 itself was actually barely positive over the decade (when dividends are included). You would never know it when looking at the advertisements from mutual fund companies.

The reality is that whenever a money manager trading stocks in one market wants to sell their performance, ask them for the performance of all of their strategies. When you get a look at the full reference set, the outperformance of one or two models will appear to be what it is: an expected outcome when viewed as just one of many. When you look at the vast reference set of mutual funds and hedge funds, the overwhelming majority underperform, *and there is no evidence the winners will continue to win.* This is why you should always ignore the past performance of a particular investment manager and question what type of money manager would sell that way in the first place. In fact, if you are working with an advisor who actually takes into account your personal situation—taxes, state of residence, outside holdings, and so on—then the portfolio should be customized to a point that they cannot show past model performance.

A trader's past performance in any given market has little or no bearing on their expected future performance. Under most circumstances, the key to understanding why a manager has outperformed over a period of time is to simply look at the field. If a small minority of professional traders are all that beat the S&P 500 over 10 years, that is not an argument in favor of hiring those managers, but rather a great example of a field full of carnage, where an intelligent investor should avoid the active manager in the first place.

Misunderstanding #2—Believing the Financial Media Exists to Help You Make Smart Decisions (a.k.a. the Media Is Killing You)*

Do you know what investing for the long run but listening to market news every day is like? It's like a man walking up a big hill with a yo-yo and keeping his eyes fixed on the yo-yo instead of the hill.

—Alan Abelson

---

*A special note to all you English majors: Yes, we are aware that "media" is plural and therefore using "the" before media is not necessary, and even considered incorrect. We researched this a bit and have found "media" widely accepted in the singular for several decades. We also think it just sounds better than saying "media is killing you." Since we have space, here is our defense:

The etymologically plural form media is often used as a singular to refer to a particular means of communication, as in The Internet is the most

It seems that no matter which direction the market is heading, there is always a chorus of vocal fatalists that dominate the financial media.

Of course, this is nothing new. Financial media have been selling fear dating back to the 1907 crash. Many books have been written citing how incorrect the financial media have been about its more recent predictions, such as the 1970s stagflation, the 1987 crash, the tech bubble (which took hysteria to an entirely new level since it accompanied the rise of 24-hour televised financial news), 9/11, the 2008 crisis, and the European debt crisis.

Every bear market has given way to a bull market. Every economic contraction has given way to economic expansion. One would think that the financial media would be reassuring during a time of crisis, especially since there is one about every three to five years. So, why is that not the case?

During any crisis (debt ceiling crisis, fiscal cliff, European debt, whatever), many pundits will encourage viewers to go to cash and many money managers will do just that, all with the purpose of "protecting" assets. Instead, anyone who follows the advice often permanently loses out on gains as the crisis subsides. And so it goes.

---

exciting new media since television. Many people regard this usage as incorrect, preferring medium in such contexts. People also use media with the definite article as a collective term to refer not to the forms of communication themselves so much as the communities and institutions behind them. In this sense, the media means something like "the press." Like other collective nouns, it may take a singular or plural verb depending on the intended meaning. If the point is to emphasize the multifaceted nature of the press, a plural verb may be more appropriate: The media have covered the trial in a variety of formats. Frequently, however, media stands as a singular noun for the aggregate of journalists and broadcasters: The media has not shown much interest in covering the trial. This development of a singular media parallels that of more established words such as data and agenda, which are also Latin plurals that have acquired a singular meaning. (*The American Heritage Dictionary of the English Language*, 4th edition, 2000)

The financial media can not only cause an investor to make significant financial mistakes, but can also cause tremendous personal stress.

A large part of the issue with financial media is that many misunderstand the purpose for its existence. Media is business, and businesses exist to make a profit. The primary purpose of CNBC, FOX Business News, CNN, and your local radio station is not to inform; it is to make money. They exist, quite simply, to make a profit.

The profit is made by selling advertisements. The ads are sold at higher prices on shows and stations with higher ratings. Because of this, the primary purpose of any financial show is to get as many viewers as possible (they call them "eyeballs") and to get those viewers to watch for as long as possible.

The rough math is:

$$\text{More viewers} = \text{higher prices for commercial space}$$
$$= \text{larger profit} = \text{happier shareholders}$$

To get the viewers, shows often overdramatize and draw out events. Many events are packaged into stories with a tag line, story line, and story arch. Often, it is accompanied by what screenwriters call "putting a clock on it."* Just as a movie will create tension and a sense of urgency with a ticking clock ("If Sandra Bullock doesn't get to the space station in 90 minutes, she will get hit by space junk and die!")† so too the financial media matches many of these stories with a clock in the lower right-hand corner of the screen. Tick, tick, tick. Just think of the "The Sequester," "The Fiscal Cliff," and so on. For a recent example, recall the clock winding down, by the minute (really, we need by the minute?) to the

---

*Thanks to my brother, Mark, a screenwriter, for sharing this concept with me. For free.

†This is a reference to the 2013 blockbuster *Gravity*, and not to be confused with "If Sandra Bullock doesn't help disarm a bomb on this bus before it drops below a certain speed, everyone will die!" which would be a reference to the 1994 blockbuster *Speed*.

Debt Ceiling limit. To further tie viewers to the set, producers and hosts will often press guests for short-term market calls.

We are not saying these events do not exist. They just tend to be developed into soap opera–type story lines. Investors often panic and make mistakes. Even more viewers get completely stressed out. How many retirement plans were messed up when some viewers went to cash during the fiscal crisis, the government shutdown, or the debt ceiling talks?

Well, now there are indications this is not all theory. In a recent study titled "Financial News and Client Stress," Dr. John Grable of Kansas State University and Dr. Sonya Britt of the University of Georgia show that *an individual's stress level increases substantially while viewing financial news, regardless of what the financial news is about* (Grable and Britt 2012). When the market is going down, people are worried about their accounts and when the market is going up, people are upset they are not more aggressively positioned.

In fact, 67 percent of people watching financial news on CNBC, Bloomberg, Fox Business, and CNN showed increased stress levels. *Even when the financial news was positive, 75 percent exhibited signs of increased stress* (Grable and Britt 2012).

Physicians often tell their patients to control their stress levels because stress and anxiety greatly increase the probability of sickness, disease, and even death.*

On top of that, I would like to add, it is not fun to be stressed out.

From a financial perspective, there is another side effect of stress that can cause immediate damage: People tend to make poorer decisions when they are under stress. The classic example is the investor who watches a lot of financial news and reacts in a panic, creating permanent losses in his or her portfolio. In my experience, I have noticed that those who are too busy to watch the financial media closely rarely make mistakes. On the other hand, it is not uncommon for a retiree who watches a lot of financial news to make a major trading decision with negative consequences.

---

*If you are asking, "Did Peter basically just allege that the news can kill you?" Well, if you watch too much of it and get worked up about it, then yes, I did!

No one is saying the media creates a crisis.* I am simply saying the media is not motivated to educate and reassure the viewer because that would reduce viewership. It is likely not a coincidence that one of the most interviewed economists on CNBC is the persistently ominous Nouriel Roubini. You may recall his nickname, Dr. Doom.

It is not unlike The Weather Channel, which has its regular viewers. However, nothing stirs up viewership like a hurricane or tornado. The meteorologist can hardly contain his glee, knowing ratings are very high. Unlike a hurricane, which leaves even the prepared with permanent damage on occasion, every bear market storm has passed, leaving the well-positioned and reasoned investor 100 percent intact.

This is not to say all media is bad (it is not), that all news is full of hyperbole (some is not), or that everyone who watches financial news, even lots of it, gets stressed out (just most of them). *It does mean, though, that if you are watching a lot of financial news, take a moment to ask yourself what you are getting out of it and how it makes you feel.*

More importantly, if the stress gets to you, do not let it impact your decision making or keep you from following your strategy. The key to having a successful, repeatable investment strategy is to stay disciplined, and a core component of staying disciplined is to recognize and shut out the noise.

Misunderstanding #3—Believing the Market Cares about Today

Although it's easy to forget sometimes, a share is not a lottery ticket . . . it's part ownership of a business.

—Peter Lynch

If a business does well, the stock eventually follows.

—Warren Buffett

---

*Actually, some people do say that, or that the media at least contribute to some crises.

People often ask the question: What makes the stock market move up or down? Some are confident that they know the answer, but they are almost always wrong.

Oftentimes, people will cite one of the following as being the primary driver of stock prices: unemployment, housing, economic policy, monetary policy, the strength of the dollar, consumer confidence, retail sales, and interest rates. All are popular choices. In order, the answer to each of these is no, no, no, still no, no, no again, no, and another final no.

The stock market cares about only one thing above all else: *anticipated earnings.* If companies make more money, their share prices eventually rise. The stock price is simply a reflection of a company's earning power. *Everything else is noise.*

Assume for a moment that you are going to buy a sandwich shop. What do you care about? The only factor you care about is anticipated earnings. If you buy the sandwich shop, you are doing so because you believe the profits earned will justify the purchase price with a good return.

To arrive at this conclusion, though, you will look at other factors that will affect your ability to make money owning this sandwich shop. For example, if interest rates are low, you will be able to make lower payments on your loan, thus making the shop more profitable. In this case, interest rates matter only because they affect your anticipated earnings. Commodity prices will also likely matter, as oil and food are commodities. If oil prices go up, it will cost more to have the food delivered to your shop every day. Rising food costs increase your expenses as well. Both increases in commodity prices eat away at your bottom line, thus hurting anticipated earnings. Consumer confidence matters because if consumers think their financial world is collapsing, they will forgo your $8 sandwich and make the kids a PB&J at home. That will drive down sales, which would impact your earnings. You get the idea.

Note, however, the important word here is "anticipated." No one cares about yesterday's earnings. For example, let's go back to that sandwich shop you want to buy. You are talking to the owner, reviewing his financials, and you can see he made $100,000 each of the last three years selling about 20,000 sandwiches a year. This sounds pretty stable, so you are thinking about offering him $200,000 for his business, knowing that you can make $100,000 per year once you pay off the debt it takes to buy it. But, you are too smart for that. You notice that he sells 5,000 of his sandwiches each year to a large corporate client. That client just went out of business. If you back those sales out, the sandwich shop would be much less profitable, so you would no longer offer the same price. You are focused on the only thing that really matters: *anticipated earnings*.

The bottom line is this: All of the other factors in the economy matter only because people buying and selling stocks are trying to determine how the changes in various "indicators"—like unemployment, interest rates, and so on—will ultimately affect a company's anticipated earnings.

No one cares how much health care companies made in the past. They want to know how the new health care reform laws will impact the future earnings of these companies. No one cares if Starbucks made a million or a billion last year. They want to know if their earnings will be hurt now that McDonald's is selling gourmet coffee. No one cares how much money General Dynamics made selling military supplies to the government in the past. They want to know if military conflicts will persist, driving up future sales.

That is why when the U.S. bear market was in full swing, investors bought Walmart stock. The thought was that Walmart's earnings would likely go up as consumers moved "downstream" to buy everything as inexpensively as possible. The same reasoning drove Nordstrom's stock price down. McDonald's did fine as investors figured consumers would want to eat out on the cheap. The same logic drove down the stock price of higher-end restaurants like the Cheesecake Factory. And, of course, companies selling alcohol did just fine as people tend to drink when they are depressed (and when they are happy, which is why alcohol is considered "recession proof").

The stock market as a whole tends to move up well before a recession is over. It does not care what is going on today. It is anticipating the earnings of companies in the future. If the stock market drops, it is because investors believe future earnings will get worse. If the market moves up, it is because investors believe the economic climate is changing in a way that will enable companies to become more profitable in the future.

Of course, so many variables go into guessing anticipated earnings that the market is not always right in the very short run (even though it is always right in the long run). For example, you can buy the perfect sandwich store in perfect conditions and then have a multitude of surprises derail your profits, like a crime in the area, unforeseen road construction blocking access to your shop, and so on. Likewise, we can have a nearly perfect economic environment, and someone can fly a plane into a building and turn everything upside down overnight.

However, unlike your sandwich store, which can go to zero, the stock market itself is resilient. Every time in history, no matter how bad things have appeared, U.S. companies as a whole have ultimately found a way to not only make money, but to make more money than they did before. Every single time. And, as always, the stock market will continue to follow the earnings.

Misunderstanding #4—Believing an All-Time High Means the Market Is Due for a Pullback

Stock Market Hits All-Time High. Now What?
                                                        —CNBC.com, April 10, 2013*

I think the market is a little frothy and I have cashed out all my positions.
                                        —Steve Grasso, Director of Institutional Trading
                                                at Stuart Frankel, in the same article

---

*The stock market has hit more than 50 all-time highs since then. All of these "events" have been accompanied by commentators talking about things like "being overdue for a correction," the market being "frothy," how it's time for a "pullback," and the like.

Don't get scared because of an "all-time high."

Whenever the market breaks through to a new high, there is talk of a bubble. Every time any market moves into new territory, the talk of a correction or bear market gets more and more incessant. You can count on it. Watching and reading the coverage regarding the Dow passing any landmark can make one's head spin.

One point of view is that once the Dow passes a "barrier," the average investor will jump back into the market and professional traders who have been sitting the market out will have to get back in, both driving the stock market much higher.

The more common slant is that the Dow, having plowed through a new threshold, is ripe for a pullback. The market, they argue, has come too far, too fast. Both crowds don't understand that Dow 10,000, 12,000, 15,000, and 18,000 are just numbers, and for the most part mean nothing. The latter crowd is also largely comprised of the "investors" who sat in cash while they contemplated the pullback that would accompany the previous Dow threshold breakthrough.

First, simply because a market is at a new high does not automatically qualify it as a "bubble." A bubble is when an asset class trades at a level far beyond its intrinsic value. In the not so distant past, we have watched a few bubbles burst. One was the tech bubble, when tech stocks were trading approximately 5 times higher than their historical valuation level and another was real estate, which was trading at more than 50 percent above its historical valuation level when it finally burst.

So, to determine if the U.S. stock market is in fact a bubble, we need to understand how stocks are valued in the first place. As with all asset classes, there are many ways to value stocks. However, the most referenced calculation is the P/E ratio. The P/E ratio is calculated by taking the stock price and dividing it by the company's earnings. For example, if a stock is at $100 per share and the earnings are $5 per share, then the P/E ratio is 20. Stock prices can go up and the market can keep hitting new highs but remain fairly valued.

To illustrate this concept, let's step into the real estate market for a moment. Let's say that the typical residential real estate investment yields an investor 10 percent. An investor searches the market and finds a duplex to buy for $100,000. The investor rents out the duplex and after paying his taxes, maintenance, and insurance, makes an annual profit of $10,000. The investor is making 10 percent and is quite happy.

A few years go by, and the economy has recovered a bit. Renters can afford to pay more, so the investor charges more rent, and his annual profit is now $15,000.

A new investor comes along and wants to buy a property to earn the typical residential real estate return of 10 percent. The new investor pays the previous owner $150,000 for his duplex. This makes sense as the profits are $15,000, which will net him 10 percent.

The duplex went from being worth $100,000 to being worth $150,000 because the earnings went up. While the price is up 50 percent, the expected return is still the same. Had the duplex gone up in value from $100,000 to $150,000, with the profit staying at $10,000, we would have a "bubble," meaning the price of the investment is much higher than the historical average. Bubbles tend to end badly. They always eventually burst. A bubble is not defined by rising prices alone; rather, a bubble is defined by rising prices relative to earnings.

The stock market does not sort of work like this; it works exactly like this.

The stock market showed us a case study of this during its ride from Dow 10,000 to Dow 13,000. The Dow was a better value on a P/E basis at 13,000 than it was at 10,000. Back when the Dow was at 10,000, the market was trading at 15.4 times earnings. When it was at 13,000, the market was trading at 15 times earnings. In other words, by this measure, the market was a better value at 13,000 than it was at Dow 10,000.

To understand how the U.S. market can come so far and still be trading at historical norms, we need to look back about six years. On October 9, 2007, the Dow was at 14,164. The path to 16,000 was a whopping total gain in the Dow of less than 13 percent! The annualized return from then to Dow 16,000 was 2 percent per year! Over the same time period, the companies that made up the Dow had seen their earnings skyrocket.

It is also important to remember that it does not matter how high a stock price goes; rather, it is how high it goes relative to its earnings. A company making $10 million per year with a share price of $100 may one day go on to make $15 million per year, at which point no one should be surprised if the stock trades at $150.

Finally, of note is that the market hits all-time highs all the time, more often than once a month on average. This should not surprise anyone either. Inflation alone is responsible for a portion of the gains. As I type this, I am drinking a Diet Coke, currently selling at an all-time high. I wish I could eat a candy bar as well. They too are selling at all-time highs. If you purchased this book* through the mail, it will have been mailed with stamps that are also priced at an all-time high. Most everything is at an all-time high most of the time, whether it is a meal at McDonald's, a car, or the cost to build a house. When you go buy your turkey for the holidays, it will likely not be selling at an all-time low. Same goes for your new car, new shirt, or new jewelry.

While the Dow flirting with thresholds is a psychological threshold, ultimately it means nothing. Market prices, like all investments, ultimately follow earnings. And for the long-term investor, that is all that matters. The next time you read that the market has hit an "all-time high," shrug and smile. It's nothing to panic about.

Misunderstanding #5—Believing Correlation Equals Causation

A black cat crossing your path sometimes signifies an animal is going somewhere.
—Groucho Marx

Just because something happens often, or appears to maintain a pattern, does not mean that there is an actual cause and effect taking place. Scientists, doctors, and statisticians learn in introductory classes that "correlation does not mean there is causation."

---

*Thank you!

For example, there is a predictive measure known as the "Super Bowl Indicator." The stock market tends to do well when the NFC wins and mediocre when the AFC wins. This indicator has been about 80 percent accurate. Nevertheless, its value going forward as an indicator is 0 percent.

There is also a predictive measure known as the *"Sports Illustrated* Swimsuit Edition Indicator." When the cover model is American, U.S. stocks tend to perform better than their historical average, and when the cover model is not American, U.S. stocks tend to perform worse than their historical average. While this has resulted in quite remarkable results with more than a 6 percent per year difference in returns, the value of this indicator is of course worthless as well.*

While we can have fun with this sort of stuff, no one takes it seriously. Or do they? Let's look at a few popular recurring stories.

October Is the Worst Month to Invest

October: This is one of the peculiarly dangerous months to speculate in stocks. The others are July, January, September, April, November, May, March, June, December, August, and February.

—Mark Twain

I met with a prospective client in late September who wanted to wait to invest his account until November because of articles he had read about how poorly stocks perform in October.

Almost every month the financial media release stories about the historical trends of a particular month. A 2012 CNN article went over all the terrible things that have happened in the market during October (Voigt 2011).

These articles reiterate a perception that there are "good times" and "bad times" to be invested, and that some easy rules of thumb—like not investing in the market in October—can be followed to achieve better returns.

---

* Other than having an excuse to look at the *Sports Illustrated* swimsuit edition for business purposes.

Unfortunately, it is just not that easy. These articles are classic examples of the media giving investors data that actually makes them less knowledgeable about investing than before they took the time to read the information.

Even if the October pattern were relevant, it sure does not hold much water. Articles on why not to invest in October state that the pattern looks really reliable if you leave out certain time periods. This is the equivalent of saying that the Rangers would have won the World Series had they won one of the last two games, or that President Obama would have lost to Senator McCain had McCain just won California, New York, and Florida. You cannot just leave out entire pieces of a data set as if they are irrelevant exceptions!

Sell in May and Go Away

Market timing does not work, at least not using Sell in May and Go Away. *As with most market-timing strategies, a little bit of analysis often reveals the devil in the details.*

—Rick Ferri, *Forbes* (2013)

The "Sell in May and Go Away" theory holds that investors should sell their stocks at the beginning of May and re-enter the market at the beginning of November. This theory is promoted on the idea that the market has historically performed better during the November through April six-month period than the May through October six-month period.

It is true that historically the stock market, at first glance, has had a better return during the November through April time period. But does this correlation imply causation? Many people believe it is real and persistent, arguing that traders take the summer months off, while another theory posits that investors receive much of their money at year end or in the beginning of the year and invest it. For our purposes, let's assume that yes, we believe that this anomaly will persist.

A recent study by CXO Advisory Group looked back at a 142-year period of the market ending in 2012 (CXO 2013). The return of a simple buy-and-hold strategy dramatically outperformed the "Sell in May" strategy. The gap is much higher when portfolio friction, the impact of costs, are included. One major factor? The "Sell in May and Go Away" proponents seem to ignore dividends* when comparing the returns of being in Treasuries during the "Go Away" period to the total returns of stocks. Because stocks do in fact pay dividends, even in the worst of times, they must be included in a fair analysis of the strategy. As is often the case, even the most cursory examination of a market "rule of thumb" will often disprove or greatly diminish its actual probability of success.

Misunderstanding #6—Believing Financial News Is Actionable

Stupid is as stupid does.

—Forrest Gump

The overwhelming majority of financial news is just noise. Part of being a successful investor is filtering out the noise as much as possible. A great example of this is how financial media will create, often out of thin air, an explanation for minor market movements.

For example, if the Dow is at 16,000 and closes the day up 50 points, it may sound like a decent-sized move, but it's not. It is a move of just .003, or less than one-third of 1 percent. This sort of move is normal, expected, and occurs because nothing substantive has happened. Nonetheless, the financial media needs to report on the day and will create a headline to explain the change. They will select from any of the day's announcements and backfill a headline. For example, a headline might read "Stocks Up on Housing Report" or "Stocks Up on Middle East Talks." If the move is just 50 points, there is really no explanation needed.

Let's say you run a chain of sandwich shops† and you sell an average of 16,000 sandwiches per day. Now, let's say that today you sold 16,050.

---

*Why is it that those who want to scare people out of the market or promote market timing leave out dividends? All that matters with any investment is the total return, which is capital appreciation *plus* dividends or income.

†Here we go with the sandwich shops again!

Is there a reason? Are you going to examine all the things you did right today to sell 50 more sandwiches or do you consider it perfectly normal variance? If instead, you sell 15,950 sandwiches, are you going to look for the reasons why? Perhaps someone should be fired? Maybe you should remodel the stores? Of course not, because selling 50 sandwiches more or less on any given day is perfectly normal. In fact, selling 100 sandwiches more or less any given day is also perfectly normal and would not cause you to blink, even for a moment.

Now, if you sell several hundred (more or less) sandwiches, perhaps something else is going on that merits investigation. It's the same with the stock market. The reality is that most market movements require no explanation. They just happen. The market doesn't close exactly where it opened very often, just like a chain of sandwich shops that sells an average of 16,000 sandwiches a day rarely actually sells that many on any given day. It's almost always more or less.

Just for fun, read the headlines on your favorite financial media site at the end of the day, and watch how they will often backfill a headline to explain statistically insignificant moves in the market. They have no choice really. Can you imagine logging on to see CNBC and reading the headline "Nothing Big Happened Today; Check Back Tomorrow"?

Misunderstanding #7—Believing Republicans Are Better for the Market Than Democrats

The common viewpoint is that Republicans are good for . . . the economy. Meanwhile the common view of Democrat policies is that they . . . are economy killers. Well, for those who feel this way, it may be time to review . . . economic history.

—Adam Hartung, *Forbes* (2012)

Most investors equate a Democratic victory as synonymous with a stock market downturn. History tells quite a different story. When the presidency transfers from a Republican to a Democrat, the stock market averages a 22.2 percent return in the inaugural year. When the presidency transfers from a Democrat to a Republican, the market averages a 6.6 percent loss in the inaugural year. CMC Market's 2012 report, "U.S. Market Performance Since 1900: Republicans versus Democrats," shows that across all terms, Democrats posted an average yearly return of 15.31 percent while Republicans fared far worse, averaging just 5.47 percent per year (Cieszynski 2012). A separate *New York Times* study compares the two from 1929 to 2008, with Democrats averaging 8.9 percent and Republicans just 0.4 percent per year. The margin has widened even more since then given the performance of the stock market since the start of President Obama's first term (McCall 2008).

There are two main theories for this traditionally unexpected result. The first theory is that investors expect radical changes from Democratic presidents, including significantly higher taxes on income and investments, corporate taxes, and an environment generally less friendly toward corporations. The same theory holds that investors expect tax cuts, spending cuts, and fiscal restraint from Republican presidents. The stock market adjusts in advance of the expected outcome of the election. When a Democrat replaces a Republican, the market often adjusts upward when it realizes that the new president may be friendlier than originally expected toward corporations and high income tax payers. Likewise, the market often adjusts downward when it realizes that the new Republican president may not cut spending as expected. Proponents of this theory cite two recent examples: (1) tax cuts, free trade, and record surpluses under President Clinton and (2) record spending and deficits under President George W. Bush. The point is simply that the market has certain expectations from each party, and many times those expectations are not fulfilled, for whatever reason.

The second theory is that this statistic is irrelevant, and has more to do with the "luck of the draw" than with whoever is President (much in the same way the stock market tends to go up if the AFC wins the Super Bowl and decline if the NFC wins).

We do know with certainty that the market is constantly "pricing in" hundreds of variables—from the deficit to interest rates; the business cycle to commodity prices; from consumer confidence to corporate profits; and yes, whoever controls the White House and Congress.

As a result, we cannot put too much emphasis on one factor alone having such a large impact on stock market performance. In total, an election itself will not drive the markets.

Misunderstanding #8—Overestimating the Impact of a Manager

Among the smaller duties of life I hardly know any one more important than that of not praising where praise is not due.

—Sydney Smith

Asset class selection is responsible for 88 percent of the investor's return, yet investors tend to give too much credit or blame to any given manager for their performance (see Figure 3.1).

In any given year, the top performing and worst performing funds tend to be in the same category. For example, in 2013, small-cap U.S. funds performed extremely well, up 30 to 45 percent. Gold funds were down substantially during the same year. Were the U.S. small-cap

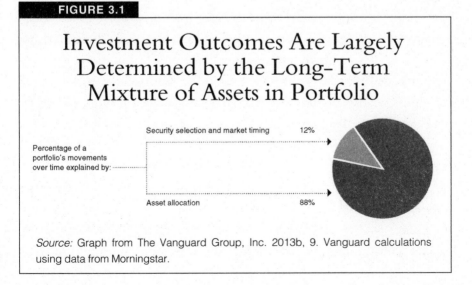

FIGURE 3.1

Investment Outcomes Are Largely Determined by the Long-Term Mixture of Assets in Portfolio

Percentage of a portfolio's movements over time explained by:

Security selection and market timing   12%

Asset allocation   88%

Source: Graph from The Vanguard Group, Inc. 2013b, 9. Vanguard calculations using data from Morningstar.

managers geniuses? No. The small-cap U.S. index outperformed most of them. They simply happened to manage U.S. small-cap funds in a year when the asset class did well. That same group performed quite poorly in 2008 when U.S. small caps were hammered. Were the gold managers complete idiots? No. They just happened to manage gold funds in a year when gold performed far worse than normal (and that is saying something, since it's normally not great to begin with). These same managers looked like geniuses in 2008.

The reality is that when looking at performance, an investor must remember two important things: (1) Regardless of how the manager performed, the odds are very high they will lose to the index going forward, and (2) even if the performance is great, most of the return is indicative of how the asset class performed, rather than due to the manager's skill. The manager, for the most part, is along for the ride.

Misunderstanding #9—Believing Market Drops Are the Time to Get Defensive

The stock market is the only thing people prefer not to buy when it is on sale.
—Original Unknown

When the market is dropping, all of the powerful forces we cover in this book, from the media to your behavioral instincts, will encourage you to take action to protect your portfolio. This usually means "getting defensive" by going to cash or switching your allocation. This is a monumental mistake—one of the worst an investor can make. As we covered exhaustively in Chapter 1, this simply doesn't work over time, and causes more harm than good. Your reaction to a market drop should be the exact opposite. If you like the market at 16,000, you should love it at 10,000.

Your asset allocation should be a function of your goals. If 60 percent of your portfolio is in stocks, and the market drops 20 percent, you should buy more stocks to get your portfolio back to its target allocation. Selling stocks is abandoning the plan at the worst possible time.

Stocks seem to be the one thing that no one wants to buy when they are on sale. If your favorite restaurant offers everything at half off, you will eat there more. If your favorite car is for sale for half off, you will quickly buy one. If a grocery store cut the price of everything by 50 percent, you would go on a shopping spree. When stocks get cut in half, investors freeze and do nothing, or even worse, sell. Instead, they wait for the prices to double, and then they want to buy! Ignore all the prognosticators who are tempting and even encouraging you to panic and make a poor decision. Remember, everything is on sale. The time to buy is now.

Avoiding Mistake #3—Misunderstanding Performance and Financial Information

The greatest enemy of knowledge is not ignorance, it is the illusion of knowledge.
—Daniel J. Boorstin, *The Discoverers: A History of Man's Search to Know His World and Himself*

A large part of the financial information an investor encounters is worthless, damaging, or misleading. For investors to protect themselves from taking action based on this sort of information, they must understand how reference sets work, understand that performance data can be misleading, view financial news with skepticism, and most importantly, *develop a skill for filtering out the noise.*

Letting Yourself Get in the Way

The most important quality for an investor is temperament, not intellect.

—Warren Buffett

Most people who get excited about investing dive into research, read market timing or stock pick letters, use online services, and watch financial news all the time. The idea is that the more they know, the better informed they will become, and the less likely they will be to make a mistake. It doesn't really work out this way. If you have a reasonable level of intelligence and you understand the basic principles of this book, you will likely outperform the great majority of investors. The key is to not mess things up. Unfortunately, there are plenty of ways to do just that. So far, we have examined strategies that are likely to do far more harm than good, but there is nothing I have personally seen cause more financial destruction than the emotionally driven mistakes investors make. The key is to recognize your behavioral biases so that you can knowingly protect yourself from making mistakes. Let's dive in.

Fear, Greed, and Herding

Fear has a greater grasp on human action than does the impressive weight of historical evidence.

—Jeremy Siegel

The fact that people will be full of greed, fear, or folly is predictable. The sequence is not predictable.

—Warren Buffett

FIGURE 4.1

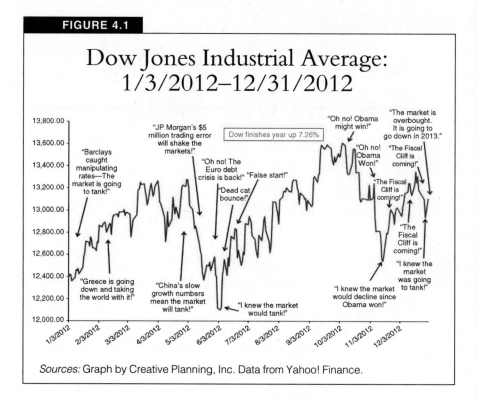

Dow Jones Industrial Average: 1/3/2012–12/31/2012

Sources: Graph by Creative Planning, Inc. Data from Yahoo! Finance.

A typical year in the market (see Figure 4.1) . . .

As humans, fear and greed are two of our ugliest traits and most powerful forces. They can impact the way we live our lives, and they can have very negative consequences for investors. Novice investors fall prey to it, legendary investors know how to control it, and the media and market prognosticators feed into it. Those two emotions, combined with our natural bias toward herding, can cause major investment mistakes.

Humans are hardwired to move in herds, to follow the crowd, and to find safety in consensus. If the market is going down and the media, commentators, and our friends are yelling "head for the exits," our herding instinct, coupled with the powerful force of fear, is to do the same. If the market is rallying, and everyone is saying "full steam ahead," our herding instinct, coupled with the alluring force of greed, entices us to join the crowd. The herding instinct can be very costly. From 1984 to 1995, the S&P 500 was up 15.4 percent per year and the average mutual

FIGURE 4.2

Mutual Fund Cash Flows
Often Follow Performance

			Investor Cash Flows over the Prior Two Years (in millions)		Stock Market Performance (cumulative)	
	Date	Equity Weighting	Stock Funds	Bond Funds	Prior Two Years	Subsequent Two Years
Early in 1990s bull market	1/31/1993	34%	—	—	—	—
Bull market peak	3/31/2000	62	$393,225	$5,100	41%	−23%
Bear market bottom	2/28/2003	40	71,815	221,475	−29	53
Bull market peak	10/31/2007	62	424,193	173,907	34	−29
Bear market bottom	2/28/2009	37	−49,942*	83,921*	−51*	94

*Reflects cash flows starting when the bear market began, rather than for the full 24 months.

Notes: Equity allocations reflect the cumulative assets under management for all U.S.-domiciled open-ended mutual funds and ETFs. Cash flows represent net cash moving in or out of stock and bond funds. Market returns are based on the MSCI USA Index through May 1994 and the MSCI USA Investable Market Index thereafter.

Sources: Graph from The Vanguard Group, Inc. 2013b, 6. Morningstar for equity allocations and cash-flow data; Thompson Reuters Datastream for market returns.

fund was up 12.3 percent per year. Over the same time period though, the average investor was up only 6.3 percent. Why? Because the investors exit underperforming markets and buy other markets doing well, constantly herding into the wrong place at the wrong time. In fact, this is what happens in nearly every significant bull and bear market (see Figure 4.2).

Unfortunately, these instincts cause the investor irreparable damage. Despite the market's insistence on going up for over 100 years, investors consistently mess up the inevitable gains by falling prey to some of the most powerful forces of human nature. In bear markets, investors have been net sellers when in fact, had they simply done nothing, they would have had substantial gains, regardless of when they bought. A more sophisticated investor is better served to take the opportunity to buy more. This is often referred to as opportunistic rebalancing. During substantial market drops, the smart investor is selling off bonds and buying stocks. With patience, this strategy has put the investor in a better place, every time. Warren Buffett has historically held his positions and aggressively added during periods of investor hysteria. He has said to "be fearful when others are greedy and greedy when others are fearful." His words are gospel for the investor trying to control the seductive pulls of fear, greed, and herding.

In a 2014 interview, former Federal Reserve Chairman Alan Greenspan reflected back on all he had learned. Interestingly, rather than lots of economic analysis, he shared his observations of human behavior saying,

> If you can grit your teeth through and just disregard short-term declines in the market or even long-term declines in the market, you will come out well. I mean you just stick all your money in stocks and go home and don't look at your portfolio you'll do far better than if you try to trade it. The reason that's the case is this asymmetry between fear and euphoria.* The most successful stock market players, the best investors, are those who recognize that the asymmetric bias in fear vs. euphoria is a tradable concept and can't fail for precisely this reason. So there are stabilities here which are very important, but along with them are more junk statistics, more junk analysis, and more stock market letters than should be allowed to be written. It's just sort of ridiculous. (Fox 2014)

It is interesting that over his entire career, Greenspan essentially learned that most everything is noise, and the strongest distinction he found among those who performed the best were that they were never scared into selling, and embraced the opportunity to buy when others were fearful. Greenspan is basically endorsing only one tradable concept: the fear and greed trade. Control your fear, control your greed, avoid the herd, and things will work out. That's some pretty interesting insight from the person most people considered the most powerful person on earth for much of his tenure.

---

*Mr. Fancy Pants is using the word "euphoria" in place of "greed." Same idea.

Dr. Frank Murtha, co-founder of MarketPsych, a behavioral economics consulting firm, said, "Investing is stressful, and that stress causes us to make emotional—usually fear-based—decisions during difficult market periods" (Fidelity Viewpoints 2013). He goes on to say that fear-based decisions impede reaching financial goals because they are focused on emotional, not financial needs, namely the desire "to feel in control again" (Fidelity Viewpoints 2013). Few things scare investors more than watching their portfolio go down day after day, week after week, and month after month. When we look back on corrections and bear markets with charts, they don't look so bad. Living through them is a completely different story. The lack of control, the idea that the portfolio is deteriorating and one can't do anything about it, causes investors to panic and sell. This makes them feel like they are in control again. The reality is quite the opposite. The market just kicked their butts. If you do this over and over, you will lose the game.

Rather than be fearful and sell out at the worst time or get greedy when the market is way up, investors should control their emotions and not only avoid panic, but embrace the market volatility for what it is: *an opportunity and a gift*. Suffocate the instincts that want to make you a bad investor and rather embrace the chaos that normally causes them to rise to the surface.

The Overconfidence Effect

Nothing is so difficult as not deceiving oneself.

—Ludwig Wittgenstein

The overconfidence effect is a well-established bias in which someone's personal confidence in their judgments is greater than reality, especially when confidence is relatively high. Let's be clear though; there's nothing wrong with confidence. That is simply trusting your abilities. Your mom wants you to be confident, your coach wants you to be confident, and I want you to be confident. Overconfidence, though, is quite dangerous as it means you are overestimating your ability to get something right. This can result in some rather poor decision making in life and investing.

In his book, *The Psychology of Judgment and Decision Making*, Scott Plous said, "No problem in judgment and decision making is more prevalent and more potentially catastrophic than overconfidence" (Plous 1993, 217). It has been blamed for lawsuits, strikes, wars, and stock market bubbles and crashes. No, he isn't exaggerating.

Psychologists Marc Alpert and Howard Raiffa conducted various studies asking individuals a myriad of questions; for example, how many foreign automobiles were imported in the United States, how many physicians were listed in Boston's Yellow Pages, and so on. The participants were told they can answer the question with as broad a range as they like, such as 1 to 1,000,000, but the range being no more than 2 percent off. Across the studies, participants averaged an inaccuracy rate of over 40 percent. Alpert and Raiffa dubbed this interesting bias of individuals to overestimate their abilities the "overconfidence effect." Since then, behavioral scientists have had a field day with the concept (Alpert and Raiffa 1982).

We now know that when someone says they are "99 percent sure" that they are actually correct about 80 percent of the time (Kahneman and Lovallo 1993). People say they are "99 percent sure" all the time. Keeping in mind how accurate they really are when they say that can help you make better decisions and make life more entertaining.*

Study after study bears out the enormous impact of the overconfidence effect: 93 percent of student drivers said their driving was above average (Svenson 1981), 94 percent of college professors think they are above average (Cross 1977), and most people think they are above-

---

* Is your spouse 99 percent sure he packed the keys to the condo? Is your son 99 percent sure he took out the trash? Are you 99 percent sure you mailed in that check? I'm 99 percent sure there are few things as fun as knowing that when someone says they are 99 percent sure of something, we know the odds they are right are 80 percent. Keep that in mind next time you are parachuting and someone tells you they are 99 percent sure they packed the parachute correctly.

average lovers† (Taleb 2007), 85 percent of people believe their future will be more pleasant and less painful for them than the average person‡ (Armor and Taylor 2002). My favorite, though, is the study of students asked about their character: 79 percent said their character was better than most, despite 27 percent of them having stolen something from a store and 60 percent of them having cheated on an exam in the previous year (Crary 2008).

The overconfidence effect has been studied and documented in the investment world more than any other area. Finance professors Brad Barber and Terrance Odean conducted a study comparing the investment performance of men to that of women (Barber and Odean 2001). They examined the trading patterns of 35,000 households over a five-year period. They found that men's overconfidence in their abilities resulted in 45 percent more trading activity than women. And what exactly did all of this overconfidence get them? The trading *reduced* their average return by 2.65 percent per year, far underperforming the women. On top of that, the men paid more in transaction fees and taxes. Overconfidence can be very expensive.

In another study, a researcher found that when analysts are 80 percent certain a stock will go up, they are right just 40 percent of the time (Van Eaton 2000). In a 2006 study, researcher James Montier surveyed 300 professional fund managers asking them to rate their performance (Montier 2006). A full 74 percent of the managers surveyed said they had delivered above-average job performance (Montier 2006, 3). Zacharakis and Shepherd found that venture capitalists are wildly overconfident with their thoughts on the prospects of success for companies they are investing in. The study found 96 percent of the venture capitalists exhibiting overconfidence (Zacharakis and Shepherd 2001). In other words, investment professionals, as a group, are very wrong at what they are supposed to do best: Measure the likelihood of a certain outcome.

---

† Admit it, you are pretty proud of yourself :)
‡ At least we are an upbeat bunch!

Richards Heuer researched the behavioral biases of CIA analysts. A key finding of his research is fascinating: "Once an experienced analyst has the minimum information necessary to make an informed judgment, obtaining additional information generally does not improve the accuracy of his or her estimates. *The additional information does, however, lead the analyst to be more confident in the judgment, to the point of overconfidence* [emphasis added]" (Heuer 1999, p. 52).

In a study on this effect, Paul Slovic, in conjunction with the Oregon Research Institute, studied the impact of giving additional information to individuals handicapping a horse race. First, they gave each individual 5 important pieces of information and asked for their predictions. Then they gave them each an additional 35 pieces of information. *This time when Slovic asked for their predictions, the handicappers were less accurate but twice as confident* (Slovic 1973)!

This is quite similar to the impact of additional information on investing. We know that those who gather more information feel better about their investments and trade more, and we know that those who trade more underperform more. The investor is mistaking all of the additional information they are collecting as added intelligence that will enable them to trade to their advantage. Instead, the studies bear out that the added information results in overconfidence. The overconfidence in turn results in activity in the account that is actually a waste of a bunch of time, money, effort, and stress—all to create underperformance.

Before you think you are too smart to fall victim to the overconfidence effect, note that Scott Plous' research has found no link whatsoever between intelligence and overconfidence (Plous 1993). In fact, there is substantial evidence that the more intelligent people are, the more likely they are to be overconfident. Research shows physicians, lawyers, engineers, and entrepreneurs all exhibit overconfidence in their respective fields. For example, physicians routinely overestimate their ability to detect certain diseases (Christensen-Szalanski and Bushyhead 1981), and lawyers in civil cases consistently overestimate the frequency with which their side will prevail (Wagenaar and Keren 1986). Professionals also bring this overconfidence into the investment world where they make mistakes, and they underperform (Daniel, Hirshleifer, and Subrahmanyam 1998; Odean 1998).

Overconfidence can take down the most sophisticated of investors. In 2011, MF Global, a brokerage and trading company, became one of the largest bankruptcies in history after a massive bet on European debt didn't work out. The cause of the collapse was attributed almost entirely to the overconfidence of its CEO, John Corzine, the former governor and Goldman Sachs chairman, and his team of traders. In 2012, one of the world's largest investment banks shook the markets when its traders created $2 billion of losses with a trading strategy run amok. Congress, concerned this signaled another potential 2008 crisis in the making, hauled JP Morgan's CEO, Jamie Dimon, in for Congressional hearings. The purpose of the hearings was to determine the cause of the market turmoil so it could be prevented from happening again. Members of the Senate expected to learn about complex trading algorithms, the use of derivatives, or computer malfunctions. Instead, Dimon testified that the trading loss was attributable to "complacency" that led to "overconfidence" (Kopecki, Benson, and Mattingly 2012).

When you hear someone make a big, bold market prediction, it is usually accompanied by a large dose of overconfidence. There are simply too many variables to predict short-term market movements, and anyone knowledgeable about markets would never make a bold short-term prediction. The bolder the call, the less valid the opinion.

Confirmation Bias

All can foresee the future only when it coincides with their own wishes, and the most grossly obvious facts can be ignored when they are unwelcome.

—George Orwell

Confirmation bias is the tendency for people to look for and favor information that confirms their preconceptions and beliefs and to avoid, devalue, or dismiss information that conflicts with their beliefs.

For example, a conservative may read the *Wall Street Journal*, view the Drudge Report online, and watch FOX News while a liberal may read the *New York Times*, view the *Huffington Post* online, and watch MSNBC. Both are seeking out information that usually confirms their ideas and are avoiding information that may conflict with their ideas. When was the last time you subscribed to a magazine, bought a book, or regularly listened to or watched a political pundit who challenged your views? If you are like most people, it's been a long time. In fact, you probably spend most of your time validating what you think is right.

What if I asked you to write down your top 10 beliefs on hot political and religious topics? Think of things that tend to get people worked up: guns, abortion, fiscal policy, global warming, religious beliefs, and so on. Now, do you think you are right about all 10 beliefs? If I brought to you the most prestigious and authoritative people in the world on each of the 10 topics to present their thoughts to you, do you think any of your thoughts or ideas would change? They likely wouldn't. Instead, you would likely devalue or dismiss nearly everything they would have to say.

You see, we all think we are right—and not just about some important things, about everything! And we constantly seek ways to validate what we think. *Highly intelligent people are doing just the opposite and instead are actively seeking out opposing views, challenging their ideas, and even occasionally changing their minds.**

If you want to get better at controlling this powerful force called confirmation bias, you need to recognize the little devil inside of your brain constantly encouraging you to validate your preconceived ideas. If you can't do that in life, well, maybe you can at least try to control confirmation bias when it comes to investing.

There is ample evidence that confirmation bias permeates throughout investors' decisions. For example, once an investor likes a stock, he is likely to seek out information that validates the stock. In a 2010 study, researchers showed that investors used message boards to seek out

---

* When was the last time you changed your point of view on any major topic? Be honest with yourself.

information that validated, rather than challenged, stocks they owned (Park et al. 2010). If we own a stock, we tend to look for anything that validates our decision to buy it, and to reinforce why we should keep holding it.

Even Warren Buffett said that he finds himself falling prey to confirmation bias and actively seeks out other investors who disagree staunchly with his ideas. One way to deal with confirmation bias is to ask yourself everything that can go wrong. For example, if you really like the idea of investing in a specific investment, pretend 10 years has passed and that you have lost a substantial sum of money on it. Ask yourself all the ways that might have happened. This forces your brain to go through the exercise of acknowledging or even, dare I say, welcoming adverse ideas.

Anchoring

The anchoring heuristic appears to be prevalent throughout human decision processes. . . .

—McElroy and Dowd (2007, p. 48)

In the 1970s, psychologists Daniel Kahneman and Amos Tversky identified the "anchoring" effect. Kahneman went on to win the 2002 Nobel Prize in economics. Tversky, who died in 1996, would have shared the prize. Their research opened the floodgates on a human bias that impacts all sorts of decision making.

Anchoring is a term psychologists use to explain the way the brain takes mental shortcuts to arrive at conclusions. In short, there is a tendency for us to over-rely on the first piece of information that enters our brain. This piece of information is the "anchor." Once the anchor is set, all future decisions revolve around the anchor, contaminating rational thinking. If you are ever not certain of a correct answer, most likely you will fall victim to the anchoring bias and guess an answer based on the most recent information. For example, if asked whether the population of Zimbabwe is greater or less than 20 million, you will give an answer. If then asked what you think is the actual population, you will likely give an answer somewhat close to 20 million.

Anchoring is well known by both novice and experienced negotiators. The first price thrown out in a negotiation often becomes the anchor. Marketers have seized upon the anchoring bias. You encounter it every time you go to the grocery store. In a fascinating experiment,* Wansink, Kent, and Hoch (1998, pp. 74–75) set up a display with Campbell's Soup on sale for 79 cents per can with a sign that said "No Limit." They then added a sign that said "Limit of 12 per Person." The shoppers who purchased the soup on sale without a limit bought an average of 3.3 cans. The shoppers who purchased the soup on sale for the exact same price, but with a limit of 12, purchased 7 cans. The shoppers were anchored to the number 12, assigning some meaning to it (for example, "Wow this must be a really good deal and the grocery store doesn't want me to buy a lot or they'll lose money."). There are many, many more studies on the anchoring effect. It is real, it is vivid, and many of us have been unknowing victims of it for years!

But wait, this is a book on investing. I'm sure you know where I am going though! The anchoring effect with stock purchases is often, you guessed it, your purchase price. If you purchase a stock for $50 and it is later $30, you may hold onto it until it gets back to $50, or even buy more because you think it is worth $50. If instead the stock goes from $50 to $70, you may sell the stock thinking it is overvalued because the price is so much higher than $50. Your decision making is clouded by your anchor.

Many investors fall victim to anchoring by buying a stock that has come far off its highs ("It's a bargain now!"), or not purchase a stock that has run on to new highs ("It is too overpriced now!"). The reality is often, in both cases, that the stock is priced pretty darn close to where it should be, with an equal number of buyers on one side and sellers on the other. The only reason the investor thinks it is a great bargain or overpriced is because of the direction it has moved from its past "anchor" price. With a heightened sense of awareness of the anchoring bias, you can avoid holding losers too long and selling winners too early. And maybe you can save some money at the grocery store.

---

*I have been told I am easily fascinated.

Loss Aversion

Having a long-term plan—and not casting it aside—is the key to dealing with our fear of loss (loss aversion).

—Ori Brafman and Rom Brafman
Sway: The Irresistible Pull of Irrational Behavior

Kahneman and Tversky are also heralded for their research regarding another powerful human bias, which they coined "loss aversion." Quite simply, loss aversion is the bias humans have to avoid a loss rather than make a gain. In other words, we fear losing more than we enjoy winning. Losses hurt more than the pleasure we get from gains.

Extensive research that has followed Kahneman and Tversky's studies show us that humans experience about twice as much pain from a loss as the pleasure they receive from gains.

In one study, researchers gave one group of people a pen with a $3.98 price sticker on it (Kahneman, Knetsch, and Thaler 1991). They then asked a group without the pens how much they would pay to purchase a pen, and asked the group that had the pens how much they would require in payment to sell their pen. Those who didn't have the pens valued the pens at a much lower amount. Why is this? Because those who already had a pen didn't want to "lose" by selling it for less than $3.98 and those who did not have a pen didn't want to "lose" by paying $3.98 or more. Have you been to a jewelry store lately? Have you noticed how they try to put the jewelry in your hands or try to get you to wear it? They are well aware of how loss aversion works. In this form of loss aversion, known as the "endowment effect" or "status quo effect," once you have a pen, jewelry, or whatever in your hands, it feels like it's yours, and you don't want to lose it.*

Loss aversion in all of its forms perhaps causes more damage among investors than any other group. Loss aversion is the reason investors sit in cash, despite knowing full well that they are purposefully and willfully

---

* "Let's see if this necklace fits you." "I bet this blouse would look lovely on you. Let's try it on." "How about we take the car for a test drive?"

losing the purchasing power of their money. The average money market yield has been well below inflation for decades. Despite that fact, investors are willingly losing a little each day to avoid potential losses with real investments. With a plan like this, purchasing power can be cut in half in just 24 years!

Loss aversion is the reason you won't finally give away the pair of pants that haven't fit you since 1994, the sweater that you haven't worn since 2003, and the reason you won't give away all the stuff you never use that you have accumulated in your garage, attic, and every other crevice of storage space in your house. Let it go. Move on!

Loss aversion is the reason that you hang on to a stock long after it has dropped. You don't want to acknowledge the loss, which would require you to no longer deny you made a mistake. Far better to just wait until it (maybe) recovers, right? Whenever I am talking with a client who has an investment they won't sell until it recovers, I ask them a simple question: "If you had cash instead of this stock, knowing what you are trying to accomplish, would you buy the same stock today?" The answer is almost always no, and when it is, we know the investor is hanging on only because of the loss aversion effect. Simple awareness of how our mind works and understanding the impact of loss aversion on our decision making can help us become better investors.*

Mental Accounting

Since the conscious mind can only handle a few thoughts at any given time, it's constantly trying to "chunk" stuff together, to make the complexity of life a little more manageable. . . . Instead of counting every dollar we spend, we parcel our dollars into particular purchases. . . . We rely on misleading shortcuts because we lack the computational power to think any other way.

—Jonah Lehrer, Wired.com

Richard Thaler is known for his work in the field of behavioral economics, and for identifying and defining *mental accounting*. By using

---

*And make us less likely to clutter our way onto the next episode of *Hoarders*!

mental accounting, an individual will divide their current and future assets into separate, nontransferable portions.

In a study highlighting the impact of mental accounting (Kahneman and Tversky 1984, 347–348), participants were asked the following:

Imagine that you have decided to see a movie and have paid the admission price of $10 per ticket. As you enter the theater, you discover that you have lost the ticket. The ticket cannot be recovered. Would you pay $10 for another ticket?

Only 46 percent of the participants said they would purchase another ticket.

He then asked the participants a similar question:

Imagine that you have decided to see a movie where admission is $10 per ticket. As you enter the theater, you discover that you have lost a $10 bill. Would you still pay $10 for a ticket to the movie?

Even though the economic impact was precisely the same as with the first question, 88 percent of the participants said yes, they would buy another ticket!

Under both scenarios, a participant was being asked to spend $10 on a ticket, despite essentially losing $10 earlier. The difference in the responses is attributable to the powerful effect of mental accounting. Once participants had a ticket, they assigned it to the "entertainment" column of their mental account. They had already lost their budget for the movie, so they weren't going to go over budget and buy another ticket. The latter group lost $10, not a ticket they paid $10 for. This group had not yet assigned the $10 to the ticket, and therefore was willing to purchase a ticket. The study shows that we don't view every dollar the same, even though we obviously should.

Psychologist Hal Arkes' research shows us that mental accounting is the reason tax refunds and lottery winnings are often blown quickly (Arkes et al. 1994). Mental accounting puts them in the "free money" column. We all know a dollar is really just a dollar though!

Sociologist Viviana Zelizer, referencing a study on the Oslo prostitution market, notes that the principle even applies to how those in the oldest profession on Earth spend their income (Zelizer 1994, p. 3).

Prostitutes, it turns out, use their welfare checks and health benefits to pay rent and other bills and use the money they acquire selling sex on drugs and alcohol. Mental accounting is ingrained in the human condition.

If you have ever gambled and found yourself winning, you may notice you became more aggressive when you were playing with "house money." Again, the mental accounting effect is at work. Money is money; we just account for it differently because of our human biases.

Mental accounting impacts the way we make decisions in everyday life, and is a contributor to wealth destruction among investors who fall into its trap. If an investor looks at each individual investment separately, this results in creating separate mental accounts for each holding. By doing this, the investor is far more likely to hold onto losers in any account with a loss than to wait for it to break even, and to sell off winners in the accounts with gains to "lock it in."

If you hold separate investment accounts, keep in mind they should not be judged individually, but rather as to whether they contribute appropriately to your long-term objective. By looking at the "big picture," it is far easier to judge if you are on track for your long-term goals. Looking at each holding or subaccount piecemeal can result in mental accounting that can trigger poor decision making. One way to dampen the impact of mental accounting in investing is to aggregate as many of your investments as possible into one account. This makes it far easier to make overall decisions that make sense for you, and dampens the mental accounting effect.

Recency Bias

If only the past were prologue, it would be a great thing. Returns do not persist. Good markets turn to bad. Bad markets turn to good. So the system is almost rigged against human psychology. If something does well in the past, it will do well in the future—that is not true. It is categorically false.

—John Bogle

Investors project out into the future what they have most recently been seeing. That is their unshakable habit.

—Warren Buffett

Recency bias is the tendency to project one's most recent experiences or observations into the future. This mental shortcut lets us make predictions about what will happen in the future based on what happened in the recent past. The problem is, this mental shortcut can create lots of problems for investors.

As humans, our minds are programmed to make it as easy as possible for us to make decisions. Most of the time, a pattern we see in the recent past will play out going forward. It worked great for the cavemen. If you see a dinosaur next to a certain cave three days in a row, it's probably best to avoid that cave! The world we live in also encourages recency bias in many ways.

The financial media have a chronic case of recency bias. Researchers reviewed *Fortune*, *Forbes*, and *BusinessWeek* cover stories on companies over 20 years, grouping the 549 cover stories into positive, neutral, and negative categories. Looking at the 500 days prior to each positive cover story, they found that the company featured outperformed the index by an average of 42.7 percent while those with negative coverage had underperformed by 34.6 percent. In the 500 days following the cover stories, the companies with a negative review outperformed by 12.4 percent while those with a positive review outperformed by just 4.2 percent (Arnold, Earl, and North 2007).

The recency bias is a dangerous instinct when it comes to investing, and when not controlled, can be very costly. Studies show brokers tend to recommend hot stocks that have outperformed over the previous year, but that those recommendations underperform the market in the following year. Investors tend to jump on stocks that have risen many months in a row, expecting the trend to continue.

The tech bubble and 9/11 bear markets were back to back. Many investors expected another bear must be coming and missed the recovery. The market went down almost constantly in late 2008 and 2009, causing many investors to expect the recent events to continue. Exiting the market, the investors missed out on the inevitable recovery. Whenever the market appears calm and rises steadily, money pours in from the sidelines, eager to buy once things appear stable.

Of course, markets don't work like this. In any given year, the odds are high the market will end the year positive, regardless of what happened the year before. In any given year, the odds are good there will be a correction, regardless of what happened the prior weeks, months, or years. In any given decade, an investor can expect about two bear markets, regardless of what happened the previous decade.

Recency bias worked well in some instances for the caveman, and even today helps us with some of our daily activities. Investing is one area the recency bias causes harm, not good, and unfortunately, it is where its impact is most costly.

Every week, Bloomberg asks strategists for their recommended allocation to stocks. Note in Figure 4.3 that the peak allocation to stocks was near the market peak in 2001, just prior to the Internet bubble bursting, and the lowest allocation to stocks was near the market low in 2009. These recommendations were a reflection of the analysts'

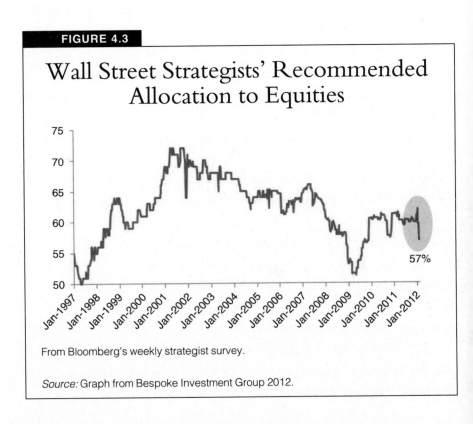

FIGURE 4.3

Wall Street Strategists' Recommended Allocation to Equities

From Bloomberg's weekly strategist survey.

Source: Graph from Bespoke Investment Group 2012.

thinking that recent events were likely to continue. In both cases they were dramatically wrong, and in both cases the damage to the portfolio of anyone following this advice was substantial. That's recency bias at work.

One effective tool to combat recency bias in investing is to follow a disciplined system for managing your money. For example, if you are in a portfolio of 70 percent stocks and 30 percent bonds, you might decide to rebalance only when the allocation changes by more than 5 percent. Another system is to set trades according to a calendar. For example, if you are exiting a large single stock position, you might exit one-fifth every month until it is diversified, so that you don't get consumed with a new decision on whether to sell each month, a decision that would likely be impacted by recent events. With a system like this, your investment decisions will be based on your disciplined process rather than on recent market events.

Negativity Bias

Brief contact with a cockroach will usually render a delicious meal inedible. The inverse phenomenon—rendering a pile of cockroaches on a platter edible by contact with one's favorite food—is unheard of.

—Paul Rozin and Edward Royzman,
Negativity Bias, Negativity Dominance, and Contagion (2001)

Negativity bias is the nature of humans to recall negative experiences more vividly than positive ones, and therefore act consciously and subconsciously to avoid negative experiences.

The negativity bias certainly helped humans survive thousands of years ago. It made sense to constantly look around for potential things that could kill you—you know, things like wild animals, crazy people with spears, and the like. Today, the negativity bias is a dead weight dragging the unsuspecting down.

The negativity bias is well documented as a powerful instinct. Teresa Amabile and Steven Kramer studied the workdays of professionals and found that negative setbacks, even if minor, were twice as powerful in impacting happiness as positive steps forward (Amabile and Kramer 2011). Researchers have also observed that learning happens faster with negative reinforcement than positive reinforcement (Haizlip et al. 2012).* Analyzing language, researchers found that 62 percent of emotional words were negative and 74 percent of words describing personality traits were negative (Averill 1980). Research even shows that negativity bias is inherent in young children, who perceive positive faces as good, negative faces as bad, but also neutral facial expressions as negative (Tottenham et al. 2013). Research tells us even babies have the negativity bias, almost proving we are "born with it" (Hamlin, Wynn, and Bloom 2010). How many times have you left an encounter with someone wondering if that person was upset with you, only because they weren't smiling the entire time? The negativity bias even affects marriage. Research by John Gottmann shows that married couples, like all of us, have positive and negative interactions, but that for a marriage to last, the ratio is five positive interactions for each negative one. (Marano 2004) Such is the force of our negativity bias.†

Our negativity bias is why the news feeds us far more negative information than good ("3 dead in heat wave!" as opposed to "Los Angeles posts best year of weather in 10 years!" or "Plane slides off runway in Chicago," instead of "There hasn't been a fatal plane crash in 3 years, a record for the industry."). It's also why during campaign season, a politician will spend far less time on his own positives, and far more time on his opponents negatives—he is feeding into our negativity bias, which resonates much louder.

For goodness sake, you must be saying, what does this have to do with investing? The negativity bias is well at work in the investment world. We know that investors feel the pain of losses twice as much as the pleasure of gains. This tilt toward the negative encourages investors suffering from negativity bias to sell during corrections—at precisely the wrong time. They would rather run to cash than experience the pain of

---

*Well, that's a bit depressing!

†Take a break and tell your spouse you love them!

the negative experience. The negativity bias is especially dangerous when there are recent events that make it more acute. This is a behavioral science term called "vividness." Some investors ride through corrections just fine, but after going through a severe bear market, such as the 2008 and 2009 financial crisis, the vividness of that experience coupled with the negativity bias becomes too much for the investor to bear, and at the slightest correction, he panics and sells at the wrong time. Vividness can create a trigger effect reaction among investors, even from the slightest market dip.

As with all behavioral biases, the best way to combat it is to be aware of it, recognize it, and squash it before the negativity bias negatively impacts you or your portfolio.

The Gambler

You've got to know when to hold 'em, know when to fold 'em, know when to walk away, know when to run.

—Kenny Rogers

We all have a gambler inside us; it's just a question of whether we can control him. Some of us are speculators, placing bets in the market and hoping for the best. Speculators include most people trading options, market timing, or placing bets on just one or two positions, all in the hope of hitting a home run or beating the market. Most of us like to think of ourselves as investors. We follow a disciplined, repeatable strategy focused on long-term investing in an effort to increase the probability of achieving our goals. Many of us, though, have a little speculating devil inside of us as well.

We all have a subconscious desire to gamble. That's why Las Vegas always finds a way to make money. Human psychology is such that if we are winning, our endorphins go crazy, and we keep playing because it *feels good*. Human psychology also encourages us to keep playing when we are losing. We keep playing for two reasons: We want to feel good again but also because we hate losing and desperately want to break even. Casinos know this, of course. They start out with the odds in their favor, but our human biases encourage us to keep playing, whether we are winning or losing, which makes sure the house odds ultimately work out for the casino. You see, the odds of winning a hand at blackjack are around 49 percent. A casino can't stay in business if people bet a hand of blackjack once or twice. The casino would lose about half the time. But, if you play a few hundred hands of blackjack, the odds are overwhelmingly against you. When was the last time you played one or two hands of blackjack, or any casino game?

The market is just as unforgiving. While the market itself goes up, the stocks within it can move all over the place, and as we know, most of the stocks underperform the market. Trading stocks also has a "house" or two that win every time: the brokerage house, which will collect a commission and the IRS, which will collect taxes. The odds that an investor will win trading stocks is the same as that of a gambler winning at the tables in Las Vegas, less than 50 percent. And as with gambling, the more times an investor trades, the more likely the odds will catch up with him and he will lose.

Have you ever noticed what your online trading platform looks and sounds like? It's green and red, with scrolling tickers, flashing images, and dinging sounds. Just like a casino. Do you think that is a coincidence?*

Avoiding Mistake #4—Letting Yourself Get in the Way

The human mind is complex, but we can't seem to shake many of our primal instincts that have been hardwired into us over thousands of years. Some of our biases can easily take over, especially those that are instinctual like fear, greed, and herding. However, all of the behavioral finance biases we have gone over here are powerful and impact the way both amateurs and professionals invest.

Remember, the market has never taken a dollar from anyone. To lose money, you have to fall prey to one of the mistakes in this book. The

---

*It's not.

top mistake people make? Letting themselves get in the way. Ultimately, it is our own behavior that does us in. The key to dodging this pitfall is to be aware of what your instincts are telling you and recognize the behavioral landmines we have covered in this chapter. Take a step back, slow down, and follow the disciplined plan you have laid out for you and your family. The car is going to get to its destination, unless you personally drive it off the cliff.

Working with the Wrong Advisor

Many investors choose to work with a financial advisor. High-net-worth investors tend to use financial advisors more than the general population. There are many different theories as to why this may be the case. Many high-net-worth households have concluded any of the following:

- They have too much to lose by making a major mistake.
- They are more likely to benefit from even minor improvements of after-tax, after-cost results.
- They are more likely to substantially benefit from noninvestment planning advice.
- They are more accustomed to utilizing professionals and paying for advice.
- They are far more likely to value their time.
- They want someone to serve as a resource to them or their family for ongoing issues.
- They want someone to provide continuity of advice in the event of an incapacity or death.

Many Americans wait until they have substantial assets and then look primarily for investment help. This is a mistake. Laying out a roadmap for success will help an investor get on the right track, pointing all efforts in the right direction. While it is true that incremental benefits do not have as much of an impact on, say someone with $100,000 to invest, it can still make a big difference toward reaching your goals if you have a strong advisor by your side. Whether you want to utilize an advisor is up to you, of course. If you are going to use one though, beware of the pitfalls.

Most Advisors Will Do Far More Harm Than Good

If you can, help others; if you cannot do that, at least do no harm to them.
—Dalai Lama XIV

Let me let you in on a big financial services industry secret: Most advisors will do far more harm than good. The vast majority of advisors fall into one of three camps:

1. They take custody of your money as part of the regular course of business.

2. They are salespeople in disguise.

3. They utilize strategies that cause more harm than good because they are trying to sell you something that you want to hear. They do this even though they know it won't work or because they don't know what they are doing.*

There are many things to look for in an advisor, but if you can navigate the three core issues of custody, conflict, and competence, you will eliminate about 90 percent of advisors, and your odds of ending up with someone competent who won't steal your money or work you over will be much higher.

Advisor Selection Issue #1—Custody

Brokerages and advisers should have independent custodians and the government should have forced me to have an independent custodian. Client funds should be held by independent custodians. If they had, I would have been caught long ago. If I had had an inspection by the SEC, they would have looked at the custodian

---

*I am so not looking forward to the hate mail I will receive from some financial advisors, but so be it.

accounts and seen the funds on my books did not match the funds in the accounts, and I would have been caught.

—Bernie Madoff (Patel 2013)

The Bernie Madoff scandal received an enormous amount of press coverage. For those not familiar with the scandal, Bernie Madoff, considered one of the nation's top money managers, admitted that he was running the biggest Ponzi scheme in history. He paid for client withdrawals out of money transferring in from new clients. The only reason Madoff was exposed is because he was faced with massive withdrawal requests from investors as the market plummeted. Because Madoff had spent or hidden most of his clients' money long ago, he didn't have any money to meet the new requests. With the stock market panic, the new deposits couldn't meet the demand for new withdrawals. With no new money left to hide the greatest financial fraud in history, Madoff confessed.

What Bernie Madoff did was despicable on a variety of levels. He not only stole money from the super wealthy and celebrities, but he bankrupted the "millionaire next door" and robbed hundreds of millions of dollars from charities and foundations. Rene-Thierry Magon de la Villehuchet, a wealthy businessman who referred clients to Madoff, committed suicide from the shame of association. Many of Madoff's former clients sold their homes and furniture. Very high profile foundations lost most of their money, and some were even forced to shut down.

The media coverage reached a fever pitch, largely because of the scale of the fraud, and because Madoff was not the only money manager stealing from clients. It is estimated that the SEC is usually investigating several hundred possible Ponzi schemes at any given time. Ponzi schemes come to light most frequently during market crashes, like 2008/2009 (see Figure 5.1). This is not because there are more crooks during those periods; it is simply because it is easier for them to get caught. During bear markets, many investors panic and ask for their money back, but because the money has been stolen and spent and no new money is coming in due to the shaky markets, the advisor is unable to meet the withdrawal request

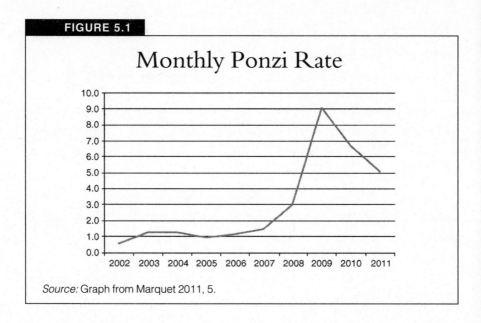

FIGURE 5.1

Monthly Ponzi Rate

Source: Graph from Marquet 2011, 5.

and is exposed. As Warren Buffett said, "It is when the tide rolls out that we see who has been swimming naked."

Some people in the media have blamed the investors for not investigating their advisor. This misses the point. How could an investor possibly have known what Bernie Madoff was doing? A background check would have shown a man who was a member of many exclusive clubs, served on the boards of charities and hospitals, and was actively involved in his religious community and causes. He gave millions to various charities, and his clients included some of the world's most sophisticated investors. Madoff even served as the chairman of NASDAQ. Yes, there were red flags. His funds were audited by a single accountant with two assistants. His investment returns, up about 10 percent every year, did not behave the way returns work in the real world. Nevertheless, it is difficult to fault the investors.

The real issue is custody. When an investor speaks with their advisor, one of the top questions that should be asked is: "Who has custody my money?"

If a client hired Madoff, he or she wrote a check to "Madoff Investments" and the money was deposited in the Madoff Investments account. This means Madoff had custody of his clients' assets. If he withdrew all the money from one investor's account and gave it to another investor making a withdrawal, no one would know the difference. Madoff's clients received reports created only by Madoff's own firm reflecting their returns (which, somehow, never went down).

The ideal way to work with an advisor is to have a separation of assets. For example, use an advisor who opens an account for you at a national brokerage firm. You can then sign a Limited Power of Attorney giving the advisor the right to place trades and bill the account only. The advisor should not have the authority to make other withdrawals. Furthermore, if your advisor provides reports to you, note that you should get the statement from the brokerage firm as well.

There are literally thousands of investment managers across the country advising clients in this manner. Because of this, it is especially imprudent for an investor to work with an advisor who insists on taking custody of all the client's investable assets.

Now, to be clear, an advisor that custodies assets at a third party can still have various forms of legal custody. For example, if the advisor is also a law firm and serves as a trustee, a trustee by definition has custody. If you are working with a trust company, for example, the trust company, by law, has custody. That is part of why you are hiring them—to entrust your funds with them rather than the beneficiary. Also, all advisors have custody to the extent that they can bill your account.

While we can slice and dice the custody rules, the point here is that your money should be held at a third party at all times. Certain types of investments lead themselves to you giving up custody of your money. These include some hedge funds, private equity funds, and real estate funds (see Figure 5.2). If you are not in a position to perform tremendous due diligence on these funds, ask yourself if you really need this type of investment.

It is fairly common for a client to bring me a "deal" and tell me that they are comfortable giving up custody because the person running the investment is at the same place of worship, from the same ethnic group, or the like. Well, that doesn't mean anything. Most Ponzi schemes (see Figure 5.3) are in fact affinity scams, where the promoter is preying on their own people, just like Madoff did.

FIGURE 5.2

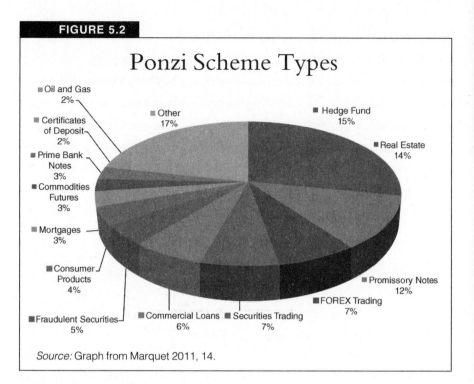

Ponzi Scheme Types

- Oil and Gas 2%
- Certificates of Deposit 2%
- Prime Bank Notes 3%
- Commodities Futures 3%
- Mortgages 3%
- Consumer Products 4%
- Fraudulent Securities 5%
- Commercial Loans 6%
- Securities Trading 7%
- Other 17%
- Hedge Fund 15%
- Real Estate 14%
- Promissory Notes 12%
- FOREX Trading 7%

Source: Graph from Marquet 2011, 14.

FIGURE 5.3

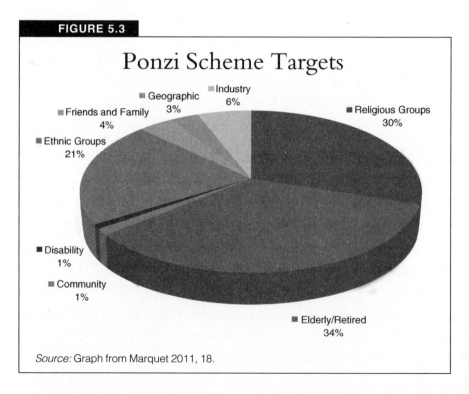

Ponzi Scheme Targets

- Industry 6%
- Geographic 3%
- Friends and Family 4%
- Ethnic Groups 21%
- Disability 1%
- Community 1%
- Religious Groups 30%
- Elderly/Retired 34%

Source: Graph from Marquet 2011, 18.

The biggest mistake Madoff's investors' made was not failing to conduct a background check, as they keep mentioning in the media. *The biggest mistake was giving him custody of all their money.* The first question you and your family should ask before entrusting everything you've worked for to an advisor is: "Who will take custody of my assets?" If the answer is the advisor, look elsewhere. If you get the right answer, *then* move on to the other important issues of conflict and competence. If you don't want someone to be able to steal your money, don't give it to them. It's that simple. Also, don't give it to an advisor who will then turn around and hand your money to hedge funds or other funds that will take custody of your money. Many of Madoff's victims didn't hire Madoff directly, but rather had paid advisors who in turn handed over custody of their money to Madoff.

Advisor Selection Issue #2—Conflict

Conflict of Interest: A conflict between the private interests and the official responsibilities of a person in a position of trust.

—Merriam-Webster Dictionary*

There are so many ways to get worked over by an advisor that it is, quite frankly, incredible. I am aware of no other industry where people go to a professional to get help and, more often than not, end up worse off than when they started. That's not a very nice thing to say, and will ruffle the feathers of quite a few in the industry, but the reality is that the financial services industry is broken. If you have a typical advisor, the odds are you would be better off without one. The reason is simple: The overwhelming majority of advisors are not on your side of the table. *They get paid more if they sell you products, they don't have a fiduciary duty to act in your best interests, or they work for a company that sells its own funds. If any of these apply to your situation, it is time to look for a new advisor, the sooner the better.*

---

*For an example, see the financial services industry.

The financial services landscape is very confusing, and this makes it easy for your advisor to mislead you. Here, I will break out this issue into three parts, to make it as easy as possible for you to determine if your advisor passes this absolutely critical test.

Test #1—Independent Advisor or Broker?

Unfortunately, only a small proportion of "financial advisors" are federally or state-registered RIAs. Most so-called financial advisors are considered "Broker-Dealers" by the Securities and Exchange Commission (SEC). Brokers are not held to a Fiduciary Standard; they are held to the lower Suitability Standard. In fact, they are required by federal law to act in the best interest of their employer, not in the best interest of their clients.

—The National Association of Personal Financial Planners, 6

Investment Advisor Defined

The Investment Advisors Act of 1940 defines a "registered investment advisor" as "a person or firm that, for compensation, is engaged in the act of providing advice, making recommendations, issuing reports or furnishing analyses on securities, either directly or through publications."

Advisors provide advice and recommendations, and are paid a fee. Investment advisors follow the fiduciary standard. *An investment advisor has a fiduciary duty to his or her clients, which means that he or she has a fundamental obligation to always act in the clients' best interests.* Investment advisors must disclose any and all conflicts of interest and are prohibited from making trades that will result in more revenue for them or their firm. Registered investment advisors are governed by the SEC.

Brokers Defined

The Securities Exchange Act of 1934 defines a "broker" as "any person engaged in the business of effecting transactions in securities for the account of others."

Brokers are paid commissions tied to investments that they select for their clients. *A broker follows the suitability standard.* The suitability standard says the broker must believe that any recommendations made are suitable for clients. A broker's primary obligation is to the firm he or she works for, not to the client, and the broker therefore does not have to place his or her interests below that of the client. Brokers are governed by FINRA.

So What's the Difference?

The bottom line is this: If your advisor is an investment advisor and governed by the SEC, then the advisor serves as a fiduciary to you, must put your interests above his own, and must act in your best interests. If your advisor is a broker and governed by FINRA, then the broker has no fiduciary duty to act in your best interests. *Why in the world would you ever pay for advice from someone who doesn't need to act in your best interests?* This is an absolutely crazy concept! Would you hire a lawyer who didn't need to act in your best interests? A doctor? An engineer? An architect? Of course not! This is the only professional field I am aware of where people seek out an advisor and pay them to *not* have an obligation to act in their best interests.

Most advisors operate under vague titles like "financial advisor." To determine if the financial advisor is an investment advisor or broker, you will need to ask questions and investigate. It won't be easy, because many advisors will try to mislead you.

As Americans have started to wise up a bit and move from brokers to investment advisors, the brokerage industry has tried to confuse the consumer further. In what became known as the "Merrill Lynch Rule," primarily because brokers lobbied for it, a proposal was put forth to allow fee-based brokers to offer financial advice that is "incidental" without registering as investment advisors with the SEC. The goal of the brokerage industry was to offer the service while still operating as a broker and without being held to the fiduciary standard. Now why would they want to do that? The reason is simple: When a broker is taken to arbitration or sued, they primarily use the defense that they have no legal obligation to act in the client's best interests. They simply "bro-kered" the transaction, much like a real estate agent brokers the sale of the house. You wouldn't sue your real estate broker if the roof caved in after you bought a home. You are responsible for making sure you have an inspection. The realtor just brokers the deal. Brokers want to use titles that make them appear as if they are on your side of the table. They use titles like "financial advisor," "financial planner," "wealth advisor," and "wealth manager." At the end of the day, a broker has no fiduciary duty to act in your best interest. They are actually lobbying Congress to keep it that way. Keep that in mind.*

The investment advisor is obligated to disclose conflicts and put your interests first. The broker is not required to disclose conflicts and puts his interests or his firm's interests first. This is an easy way to screen an advisor. There are approximately 300,000 financial advisors in the United States. Most of them are brokers. That means most of the financial services industry doesn't need to act in your best interests. Fascinating, right? Well, eliminate the brokers by asking a few questions:

1. Are you a broker or investment advisor? Correct answer: Investment advisor only.

2. Are you registered with the SEC or FINRA? Correct answer: SEC only, not both, and not just FINRA.

3. Do you have the Series 7 or 65 license? Correct answer: The 65, not both, and not just the 7.

Note that all of the above are really the same question. An investment advisor is always regulated by the SEC. A broker will have the Series 7. Now that we have narrowed the field by eliminating approximately 85 percent of the financial advisors, let's narrow the field further† (PBS 2013).

------

*Imagine this: You pay a financial advisor and he shares the fee with his firm. That firm then spends some of that money lobbying Congress to allow them to advise you without having to act in your best interests. That sums up the majority of the financial services industry, and it's totally ridiculous.

†Note that I am not saying that all brokers are bad. That is certainly not the case. There are ethical and unethical brokers just like there are ethical and unethical investment advisors. I am simply saying that you should, at a minimum, require that the person you hire to help you has a fiduciary obligation to act in your best interests at all times, and brokers don't meet that requirement.

Test #2—Pure Independent versus Independent and Broker

The dually registered advisor is the ultimate wolf in sheep's clothing.

So far we have divided the financial advisory field into two main categories: independent investment advisors and brokers. However, we need to go one more step to make sure you are always dealing with someone that must *always* act in your best interests. Some independent investment advisors are dually registered. This means that they are both an independent advisor and a broker.

This is an extremely dangerous advisor because this advisor can say they are an investment advisor and is held to the fiduciary standard and would be telling the truth. However—and this is a *huge* however—*the same person can switch from being an investment advisor with a fiduciary duty to act in your best interests to a broker who can sell you something and not act in your best interests in the same conversation.* You read that right. By dually registering, an advisor can operate under the fiduciary standard sometimes and as a broker avoiding the standard sometimes. Good luck figuring out which is which. The dually registered advisor is the ultimate wolf in sheep's clothing.

There are two ways to see if an "independent investment advisor" is also operating as a broker. First, ask. Second, look at their business card or website. If it says "securities offered by ABC broker dealer," then you are dealing with someone who is also a broker. If you are working with a dually registered advisor, don't be surprised if your investment portfolio ends up owning commissionable investments or proprietary funds (funds that the company owns).

Test # 3—Proprietary Funds versus No Proprietary Funds

It is highly unlikely that your advisor happens to work for the company that has the absolute best investment for you for any allocation in your portfolio.

Advisors who are brokers or who are dually registered often work for a company whose parent company or sister company offers proprietary funds. This means that the company owns funds, and often it will sell those funds to its clients. For example, in a common setup, an investment firm owns two sub-firms: a registered investment advisor (RIA) as well as a brokerage that owns mutual funds, hedge funds, and the like. The financial advisors are then dually registered. The advisors then market themselves as "independent advisors." The client signs an agreement they never read or wouldn't understand anyway. The "independent advisor" then puts the sister company's mutual funds, separately managed accounts, and hedge funds into the client's portfolio. Often, these funds operate under different names, making it even harder for the client to know they are being sold proprietary funds. In my opinion, *this is the worst type of setup for a client because the client has gone through the effort to seek out an independent advisor and instead ended up with a salesperson in disguise.* And make no mistake, when you hire a broker, you are hiring a salesperson, not an advisor. If you are going to pay an advisor to give you advice, the least you should ask for is that they don't have a product to sell you and that they have to act in your best interests.

You don't go to a Honda dealership and pay someone to tell you what kind of car to buy. They are going to recommend a Honda, regardless. Likewise, you should never work with an advisor whose company or affiliated company has proprietary funds. If you do, don't be surprised when they end up in your portfolio.

If you are working with a broker or dually registered advisor, take a look at your portfolio. Examine what you own. You will likely find that you own some of the funds owned by the affiliated company. Ask yourself this: Are these the absolute best funds in the world for me? The answer is no. It is highly unlikely that your advisor happens to work for the company that has the absolute best investment for you for any allocation in your portfolio. It may happen at times, but it is unlikely. If an advisor works for a company that has its own funds, or is affiliated with a company that has its own funds, move on with your search.

A Final Thought on Conflicts

I have often heard people say that although they work with an advisor who has a conflict, it doesn't matter because their particular advisor is trustworthy or because they are always checking the advice of the advisor. To those of you who feel this way, keep in mind that you might not be around one day. What sort of advice will your spouse or kids receive when you are gone? As an estate planning attorney, I have seen many instances of a surviving spouse being sold an annuity by an advisor before they even get to my office. Also, you might be around a long time but not have your wits about you for part of your life. When you and your family are facing the toughest personal struggles, it's ideal to have a financial advisor who has no incentive to do anything differently. Warren Buffett is fond of saying he likes to buy a company that can be run by an idiot, because one day it will be. I recommend always having an independent advisor who is not a broker, because while the conflict of interest a broker brings to the table may not present itself today, one day it likely may.

Advisor Selection Issue #3—Competence

Never ascribe to malice that which adequately can be explained by incompetence.
—Napoleon Bonaparte

It's quite sad that we have eliminated most advisors simply because the overwhelming majority of them have a conflict of interest. They simply are salespeople, sometimes in bad disguises and other times in very good disguises. We have now moved on to the thousands of independent advisors governed by the SEC who are not also registered as brokers. While this group has a duty to act in your best interests, they still need to be weeded out for competence and relevance.

The financial advisory field is quite different than other professions like medicine, law, engineering, education, and the like. If you want to be a doctor, you go to medical school. Lawyers go to law school. Engineers get a degree in engineering. Teachers get a degree in education. The overwhelming majority of financial advisors, I would speculate well over 95 percent, have no college education in financial planning or investment management because (until recently) there wasn't a college-level program offered. They learn it on the job. Since that is the case, how do you identify an advisor with competence and relevance?

Competence Check #1—Do the Advisor's Credentials Meet Your Needs?

As of July 2014, there are 142 professional designations on the FINRA website for the financial services industry. Most of them are worthless. If you are looking for financial planning help, be sure your advisor or someone on their team is a Certified Financial Planner (CFP). If you are seeking advanced tax advice, get it from a CPA. If estate planning is required, utilize an estate planning attorney. These designations and degrees require a college degree, advanced studies, a formal exam, and continuing education. Set the bar at least at this level.

Competence Check #2—Is the Advisor Right for You?

An advisor can be an independent advisor with no conflicts, not have any proprietary funds, have the CFP, and still not make sense for you. Be sure the advisor you choose works with people like you. If you are going to have heart surgery, you want to go to a doctor who successfully performs heart surgery all the time. If you are wrongfully accused of a crime,* you will look for a criminal defense attorney who has had prior success working with people in your situation. Likewise, when choosing a financial advisor, choose one who successfully works with people in your situation, all the time. If you are just getting started, find an advisor who works primarily with clients at your stage of life. If you are high net worth, choose an advisor who works primarily with high-net-worth households. You don't want your advisor learning at the expense of your

---

*Or not wrongfully. I'm giving you the benefit of the doubt here!

financial well-being. When an issue comes up, you want your advisor to have "been there, done that."

Competence Check #3—Is the Advisor Following a Process That You Agree With?

There are still thousands of advisors who are independent with no conflicts, don't sell proprietary funds, and work with your type of situation.* The final screen is to make sure that what they are selling actually works and fits your personal philosophy.

The financial services industry is a mess. Most advisors are not aligned with the client's best interests. Most advisors are in the business of selling something, whether it is clear to the client or not. Even those who are truly independent often sell a strategy they know people want to buy. It's easy for a financial advisor to sign on a client by telling the prospective client there is a way to participate in the upside of the market and at the same time get out of the way before a downturn. Whenever there is something people want to buy, someone will sell it. A competent and ethical advisor knows that this cannot be systemically done and won't sell it. A competent but unethical advisor knows it can't be done, but will sell it anyway.

According to a recent study, an advisor following the principles set forth in this book can provide added value of about 3 percent per year, with some years adding negligible value and others adding value of well over 10 percent, notably during periods of large market swings (Kinniry, Jaconetti, DiJoseph, and Zilbering 2014). If the principles of this book ring true to you, then you should seek out an advisor who is focused on avoiding market timing, active trading, and selling performance and instead is focused on building a plan to develop a roadmap, focused on an allocation that makes sense for you, keeping costs and taxes low, and following a disciplined repeatable approach to investing that avoids behavioral missteps.

---

*Though, sadly, the field is getting quite thin.

A Final Thought on Advisors—Principles

It's good to stand for something, believe in something, and base your business on values.

— Jerry Greenfield, Ben & Jerry's

Many advisors offer strategies like the one in this book but at the same time offer market timing strategies, tactical strategies, active trading, hedge funds, and the like. Select an advisor with principles and values. One who has something they believe in and actually implement for their clients rather than a firm with a bunch of various "products and packages" trying to compete in every space. If a firm offers an approach like the one outlined in this book, but also offers a tactical strategy, downside protection strategy, or market timing strategy, then they are telling you they will do anything to make a buck, because they are selling strategies that directly contradict each other. It doesn't matter to them if something works or not. All that matters to them is selling you on becoming a client, no matter what strategy you want. You wouldn't choose a doctor who firmly believes in one approach to healing, and believes another approach will actually harm you but would take that approach anyway.

If a prospective client comes to me looking for active options trading, hedge funds, market timing, and the like, I tell them I am not the advisor for them. I don't set up another fund to take them on. You should demand the same from an advisor. Once you determine the approach that's right for you, find an advisor who follows that approach as a matter of discipline and principle. Require that your advisor have a philosophical soul.

Avoiding Mistake #5—Choosing the Wrong Advisor

Be sure you put your feet in the right place, then stand firm.

— Abraham Lincoln

In my career, I have witnessed the unfortunate aftermath of many investment mistakes. It is always unfortunate when I see a client who blew up their portfolio. It is *tragic* when a financial advisor has caused the damage. I always feel the most sympathy for those who knew they needed help, sought it out, then ended up with an advisor who either put the client in commissionable products, sold the client proprietary funds, missed out on gains because of a stupid market timing strategy, or blew up the portfolio with an active strategy.

A good list of questions to ask your advisor will include the following:

1. Where will my money be held? Right answer: Somewhere else!

2. Are you a broker? Right answer: No!

3. Are you a dually registered advisor? Right answer: No!

4. Do you or any affiliate have proprietary investments of any kind? Right answer: No!

5. How are you compensated? Right answer: Total disclosure in writing and never make commissions on any investment product.

6. What are the credentials of you and/or your team? Right answer: If planning is involved, a CFP is ideal to have on the team.

7. What is your planning and investment management approach? Right answer: The firm should follow a coherent philosophy rather than a bunch of different strategies (unprincipled) and should follow an approach that does not involve market timing or active trading.

If an advisor is the right solution for you, make your decision carefully. Understand the importance of custody and competence, but most importantly, *make sure your advisor has no conflict and follows the investment philosophy that makes sense for you.* Put your requirements in writing, and stick to them. Do not be swayed in the meeting with a prospective advisor. Once you have put your feet in place, stand firm.

A financial advisor can greatly increase the odds of you attaining your financial goals by providing peace of mind, offering continuity of advice for your family, partnering with you to make better financial decisions, and likely helping your portfolio perform better—that is, if you have the right advisor.

Getting It Right

Knowledge is knowing a tomato is a fruit. Wisdom is not putting it in a fruit salad.

—Miles Kington

When it comes to investing, much of the game is simply not messing things up. We have covered that in detail thus far. But, of course, the goal is to not only avoid getting in the way of success; it is to maximize the odds of success.

Having gone over the key mistakes to avoid, we can move on to discuss how to optimize your results.

Rule #1: Have a Clearly Defined Plan

If you don't know where you are going, you'll end up someplace else.

—Yogi Berra

You don't start a race without knowing where the finish line is. You don't go on a hike without knowing your destination and the conditions you may encounter. You don't start driving somewhere without knowing where you are going.* Nonetheless, most investors invest without an endgame laid out in advance. Without a destination, it is easy to drift off course. Without a plan, it is easy to change the strategy midstream, increasing the odds of messing everything up.

Before you invest one dollar, you must have a plan. A plan does not need to be a 150-page road map of how you will invest every minute for the rest of your life. A plan can be very straightforward.

---

*My wife disputes this statement.

Step 1—We simply begin with determining the starting line, which is where you are today. Build a net worth statement that lays out all of your assets and liabilities.

Step 2—Then, you need to know your goal. A goal must be very specific and realistic. An example of a goal that would not work well is: "I want to retire with a lot of money." Come on, people! We need to have a clearly defined purpose. Something like this will work: "I would like to retire at age 62 with a post-tax income of $100,000 per year adjusted for inflation, and I want to assume social security will not be there for me." Now that is something we can work with!

Step 3—Run a projection showing how on track you are for that goal. There are online tools to help you do this, or your advisor can do this with you. Be sure to exclude assets that are not available to fund retirement. For example, if your net worth statement shows you have $800,000 today, but you are going to spend $150,000 on your kids' weddings and education, the projection should start with the money you have today that is available for retirement, which is $650,000 ($800,000 less the $150,000 you need for the kids). Then, include the money you are saving regularly, whether it is to your retirement plan at work, an IRA, or a taxable account. These projections can get more sophisticated if you include social security, other income like pensions or rental income, potential inheritances, and other variables. It is here that we will determine how on track you may be for your goals.

Step 4—Now, determine if you need to adjust your goal. For example, if your projection shows that to hit your goal you need to have an investment rate of return of 20 percent a year, well, change the goal, because it very likely isn't going to work out. You can adjust your goal by lowering your income need, saving more, or pushing your retirement date out.

Step 5—Once we have a starting point and an end goal, we can move on to building the portfolio. Note that your plan needs to be revisited regularly (more on this later).

You may have different plans for different portfolios. For example, you may have separate investments set aside for education. This will have a different starting amount (what you have set aside) and a different goal (the amount of education you want to fund). You may have yet another goal for a second home, a wedding fund, or a trust set aside for kids or grandkids. Each of these portfolios should be constructed only after a solid plan has been laid out, making the objectives clear.

Finally, for those with excess wealth, which means having money beyond the pool of money you need to achieve all of your goals, it is perfectly legitimate to have as your goal for the excess wealth portfolio to simply "beat the S&P 500" or anything else you may fancy.* The key is to make sure that you have a solid portfolio in place to get you on track to financial security. After that, the excess wealth can be invested in a variety of ways.

In each case, whether it is for retirement, education, excess wealth, or any other portfolio, first determine a specific goal. Everything else flows from that purpose.

Rule #2—Avoid Asset Classes That Diminish Results

There are five major asset classes: cash, commodities (like gold and energy), stocks, bonds, and real estate. I will start with the two asset classes that should never be included in an investor's portfolio, and then cover how to construct an allocation targeted toward your goals.

Cash—The Illusion of Safety

The one thing I will tell you is the worst investment you can have is cash. Everybody is talking about cash being king and all that sort of thing. Cash is going to become worth less over time. But good businesses are going to become worth more over time.

—Warren Buffett

---

* Note that we will cover how to do this later, and it won't include market timing, actively trading, or voodoo. (No offense to those of you who practice voodoo. It probably is more effective than market timing or actively trading stocks.)

When we think of risky asset classes, we tend to think of commodities, real estate, stocks, and even some bonds. Cash may be last on the list. Cash, however, has many inherent risks as well.

First and foremost, cash is the worst performing asset class in history. Over long periods of time, cash has always underperformed all other major asset classes. The more time you spend with a significant portion of your holdings in cash, the higher the probability your portfolio will underperform.

Second, holding cash for long periods of time guarantees that you will not keep up with inflation. Cash guarantees the loss of purchasing power. In essence, your cash becomes worth less and less each year as prices go up and your cash does not. Imagine you put $100,000 in the bank and earn 1 percent or so a year for 10 years. When you pick up your cash, you may feel pretty good. However, the 1 percent or so you earned did not keep up with the cost of a stamp, a suit, a candy bar, health care, or education. You may think you made money, but you lost purchasing power.

One reason many "investors" hold cash is to time the market. They do this despite the fact that there has never been a documented, real-world study done by anyone ever showing that repeatedly moving from the market to cash and back to the market works. After all, you need to be right about when to get out, then when to get in, and do it over and over again. If you get burned just once, it can be "over" and your performance permanently affected.

Finally, many investors hold cash in the event of financial Armageddon, a situation when the stock market goes to zero or near zero and never recovers. In reality, if we live in a world where Walmart, Nike, McDonald's, Exxon Mobil, and the rest of the world's dominant companies go down and never recover, it will likely accompany a default by the U.S. government on treasury bonds. How can the U.S. government make its debt payments on its bonds if the major U.S. companies have collapsed? Who exactly would be working and paying taxes to cover the debt payments? In this event, cash is worthless as the FDIC guarantee would essentially mean nothing. If you do not believe

America's major corporations can survive, then the natural conclusion is that the U.S. economic system itself cannot survive. In that event, cash may be the worst asset to own.

Despite all of this, Americans are currently sitting on more than 3 trillion in cash, the most in history. Of course, the cash peak started at the stock market bottom in 2009, at precisely the worst time.

Cash gives people comfort because, for goodness sakes, it does not move around at all. It is easy to understand, and it does not "go down." But there is more to the story than that. While cash brings comfort, it does not keep up with inflation, constantly loses purchasing power, drags down long-term investment returns, and is of no value in the event of a true economic collapse. Keeping short-term reserves on hand is a good idea. Hoarding cash as a long-term investment, not so much. Eliminate cash as a consideration for your investment portfolio.

The Illusion of Gold as a Way to Grow Wealth

What motivates most gold purchasers is their belief that the ranks of the fearful will grow. During the past decade that belief has proved correct. Beyond that, the rising price has on its own generated additional buying enthusiasm, attracting purchasers who see the rise as validating an investment thesis. As "bandwagon" investors join any party, they create their own truth—for a while.

—Warren Buffett*

In case you had not noticed, there is a gold rush taking place, with investors adding more and more of their portfolio to the precious metal.

---

*Also from Buffett, and much more entertaining: "Gold gets dug out of the ground in Africa, or someplace. Then we melt it down, dig another hole, bury it again, and pay people to stand around guarding it. It has no utility. Anyone watching from Mars would be scratching his head."

Many investors are flocking to gold as they worry that the dollar is losing so much value it may become worthless. Others worry the global economy will collapse, and gold will be the one true currency. Still others view it as the safest place to be should we see high inflation.

Unlike companies, real estate, and energy, gold itself is nearly intrinsically worthless. Companies and real estate have the potential to create income. Energy companies have the potential to produce income. Oil itself is used as one of the most critical resources in the global economy. Gold produces no income and is not a critical resource. Historically, gold has performed worse than stocks, real estate, energy, and bonds, barely keeping pace with inflation (see Figure 6.1). Every time in history it has outperformed substantially, it has ultimately collapsed. Finally, while gold has proven to dramatically underperform stocks and even bonds over the long run, it is still one of the most volatile asset classes. Gold belongs only in the portfolios of fearmongers and speculators. If you own gold in your portfolio, expect to not get paid an income, pay higher taxes on your returns, take a more volatile ride than the stock market, and get a long-term return lower than bonds. No thanks.

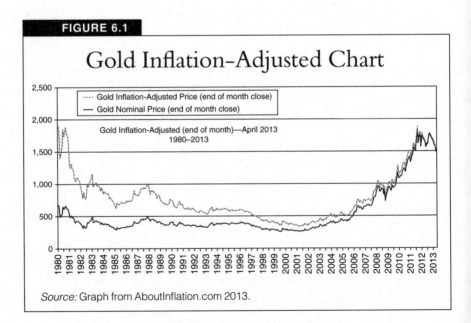

FIGURE 6.1

Gold Inflation–Adjusted Chart

Source: Graph from AboutInflation.com 2013.

Rule #3—Use Stocks and Bonds as the Core Building Blocks of Your Intelligently Constructed Portfolio

Bonds

Several studies have thoroughly documented that asset allocation is the primary driver of investment performance, accounting for 88 percent of the portfolio's returns. For example, if you own a handful of large-cap stocks, a large-cap mutual fund, or a large-cap index, you will get close to the same return most of the time. The other 12 percent of the portfolio's returns will be driven by other factors such as security selection and market timing, two factors that usually hurt performance.

Proper portfolio construction is part art, part science, and certainly never perfect, but goes a long way toward following a plan that makes sense for your particular situation. Much is made of which asset classes are "good" or "bad" when in reality it's your goals, not the various markets, that should drive the exposure to any given asset class in any given portfolio. For most, but not all, investors, owning multiple asset classes to achieve various goals makes the most sense.

Bonds deliver a positive return about 85 percent of the time. With a bond you are loaning money to a company or other entity. A treasury bond is a loan to the federal government; a municipal bond is a loan to a municipality such as a city or state. A corporate bond is a loan to a corporation like McDonald's or Nike; a high yield bond, also known as a junk bond, is a loan to a corporation that has to pay higher interest to attract investors to loan them money.

A lender is in a more predictable position than a stockholder. As long as the company stays around, the lender gets paid back with interest. A stockholder never really knows what will happen as the stock can fluctuate all over the place. *It is for this reason that, over the long run, bonds are expected to underperform stocks. You should not own bonds on the expectation they will do otherwise.* So if bonds are expected to underperform, why in the world might you buy them? Well, several reasons. First, while stocks are very likely to perform well over 10 years, there is a lot of precedent for prolonged periods of misery (see 9/11, the tech bubble, or 2008/2009 for a modern-day refresher). It is important that income needs be met for three to seven years so that the investor is never at the mercy of the stock market's often random gyrations. That way, between the bonds and their income, you can get the monthly income you need, whether or not there is a flash crash, someone flies into a building, or any other event occurs.

Basically, bonds are insurance. *We are giving up expected return in exchange for dramatically increasing the likelihood the investor's needs will be met in the short and long run.* As an example, let's say you are retiring next year, and so long as you earn 6 percent per year, you will have the $120,000 per year you want in retirement. While stocks will likely outperform bonds throughout your retirement, we know two important things: (1) Stocks may underperform bonds in the first few years of your retirement, and (2) you don't need to be 100 percent in stocks to net a 6 percent return. Because of this, you should look at owning enough bonds to cover about five years of retirement, to avoid the scenario of drawing down on a portfolio during a bear market that may appear in the beginning stage of your golden years.

Finally, while much of this book is focused on the case for indexing your stock portfolio, the bond market is a different animal altogether. There is a fair debate as to whether active management adds value in this space, so mutual funds, institutional funds, index funds, and individual bonds may all make sense to fill your bond allocation.

Stocks

Stocks are the subject of ceaseless predictions, when really they are the most unpredictable and predictable (yes, both) asset class. No one, absolutely no one, can predict the short-term movement of stock prices. As a reminder, anyone who tells you otherwise is likely an idiot or a liar (not sure which is worse, really). Yes, those are strong words, but with all the noise, it is important to understand this as it impacts the allocation to this critical asset class. Because stocks are not predictable in the short run, an investor should not own them to meet short-term needs. However, over the long run, stocks are expected to perform far better than bonds. Because stocks are riskier than bonds, they come with an implied "risk premium." If bonds were expected to perform as well, no one would ever take on the volatility that comes with owning stocks. While over the short run, stock prices are completely and totally unpredictable, over the long run, as a group, they have always done one thing: Go up. A lot.

While this inevitable outcome has persisted for over a century, the constant corrections, crashes, and day-to-day movements drive out the fainthearted or cause them to jump ship at the worst possible time. *Part of having the patience to make it through all this is to have stock market exposure only for the portion of your portfolio allocated for income needs more than five years out, depending on a variety of factors.* If you are not at the mercy of the market over the next few years, and we know over the long run the market has done nothing but go up, it becomes far easier to get through the rollercoaster ride along the way.

If any investor has more than 10 to 20 years before part of the portfolio may be needed, this can be invested in subsets of the market that are extremely volatile but have a long, well-documented history of rewarding the investor for their patience. This includes mid-cap stocks, small-cap stocks, microcap stocks, and emerging markets stocks. The higher volatility should reward the investor with a higher return. As an example, if an investor has more than 20 years to retirement, they might have a substantial part of their portfolio in emerging markets. Some investors have wealth they will never spend or parts of the portfolio they will never touch. For situations like this, it can make sense for even a 75-year-old to have a significant portion of their portfolio in small stocks or emerging markets stocks.

Buyer beware! If you cannot stand the heat, get the heck out of the kitchen. While on paper and over time this strategy works well, it is not for the fainthearted. These subasset classes are often quite uncorrelated, can move quickly, and can underperform for long periods of time. *A good way to know if these subasset classes make sense for you is your reaction to a drop.* If you get excited at the opportunity to sell off bonds and buy more small caps and emerging markets while they are getting hammered, they will work well for you. If you find yourself generally freaking out about the drops, you will not last in the position long enough for it to work out, and you will cause your portfolio undue harm.

Real Estate, Energy, and MLPs

For higher-net-worth investors, adding real estate and energy can serve as inflation hedges. The best way to buy real estate is using an indexed ETF or index fund. The best way to gain exposure to energy is by owning an energy company index ETF or index fund. Avoid holdings that own oil itself. These track the price of oil and the return can vary widely from the actual price of oil due to things like cantango and backwardation.* MLPs, or Master Limited Partnerships, can be a great fit for a high-net-worth or high-income investor, but consult a professional prior to purchasing as the investment vehicle used and the account type can greatly reduce the advantages of these unique investments. For most though, especially those who want to keep things low maintenance, a simple allocation of stocks and bonds can be far better than getting too cute with the portfolio.

The goal is to increase the probability of achieving your goals. In the end, the wealth you have accumulated is a means to an end. You have some purpose for it. The asset classes and subasset classes you own should always be tied, as closely as possible, to your goals.

Putting It All Together

The individual investor should act consistently as an investor and not as a speculator.

—Benjamin Graham

Knowing the rate of return required of the various portfolios, we can work our way to a basic allocation.

Looking at the returns, it seems to make sense to go "all in" with the stock market (see Figure 6.2). Of course, nothing is that easy. The higher

---

*Not worth explaining!

FIGURE 6.2

Historical Returns

Asset Allocation	1926–2012 Nominal Average Annual Returns
100% cash investments	3.60%
100% bonds	5.54%
80% bonds, 20% stocks	6.74%
70% bonds, 30% stocks	7.28%
60% bonds, 40% stocks	7.79%
50% bonds, 50% stocks	8.25%
40% bonds, 60% stocks	8.68%
30% bonds, 70% stocks	9.07%
20% bonds, 80% stocks	9.41%
100% stocks	9.97%

Note: Stocks are represented by the Standard & Poor's 90 Index from 1926 to March 3, 1957; the S&P 500 Index from March 4, 1957, through 1974; the Wilshire 500 Index from 1975 through April 22, 2005; and the MSCI U.S. Broad Market Index thereafter. Bonds are represented by the S&P High Grade Corporate Index from 1926 to 1968; the Citigroup High Grade Index from 1969 to 1972; the Barclays U.S. Long Credit AA Index from 1973 to 1975, and the Barclays U.S. Aggregate Bond Index thereafter. Data are through December 31, 2013.

Source: Data from The Vanguard Group, Inc. 2013b, 10.

the allocation to stocks, the more volatile the portfolio will perform. For example, a 100 percent stock portfolio has ranged from its best annual return of 54.2 percent to its worst at −43.1 percent while a 60 percent stock/40 percent bond portfolio has ranged from a 36.7 percent best to −26.6 percent worst return, a much narrower range of performance (see Figure 6.3).

Rule #4—Take a Global Approach

Investors tend to have a home country bias, meaning they invest most of their money in companies that operate out of their home country. This is evidenced all over the world. For example, Australians own a disproportionately large amount of their portfolio in home country stocks

FIGURE 6.3

The Mixture of Assets Defines the Spectrum of Returns

Best, worst, and average returns for various stock/bond allocations, 1926–2013

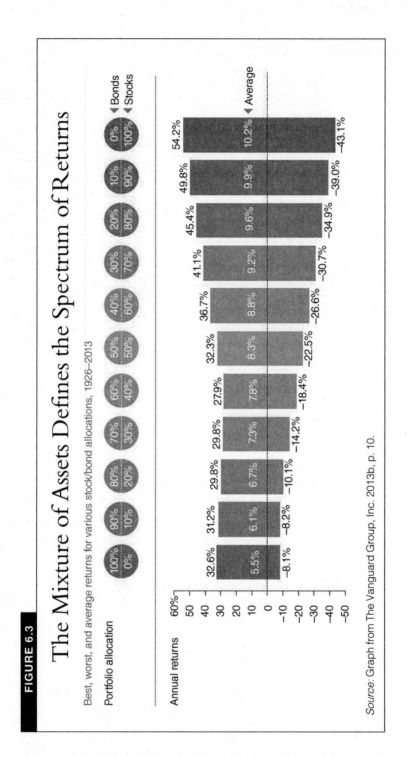

Source: Graph from The Vanguard Group, Inc. 2013b, p. 10.

as do investors throughout Europe and Asia. U.S. investors, more than any other country, can justify a home bias. This is because there is a disproportionately large share of the global economy and stock market equity that exists in the United States.

Nonetheless, U.S. investors should use international holdings as part of their portfolio for several reasons: (1) We live in a global economy and companies everywhere can and do make money; (2) international holdings often behave somewhat differently than U.S. holdings; (3) the U.S. markets and international markets often "take turns" out-performing one another for short and sometimes long periods of time; (4) the difference in returns can dampen portfolio volatility; and (5) many international economies, especially the emerging market economies, have far higher projected growth rates than the United States.

One does not need to become an international exchange expert to create a global portfolio. By simply purchasing an index fund, an investor can instantly add global exposure. For example, if your allocation targets 60 percent U.S. stocks, you can assign 1/3 of that allocation to global stocks by buying an international ETF. The same can be done with your bond allocation.

Rule #5—Use Primarily Index-Based Positions

If the data do not prove that indexing wins, well the data are wrong.

—John Bogle

As we covered in Chapter 2, actively trading securities in any asset class will likely yield lower returns. Choose index-based holdings for most if not all of your portfolio.

Rule #6—Don't Blow Out Your Existing Holdings

Know what you own, and know why you own it.

—Peter Lynch

Once you have determined the right allocation for you, work toward it as quickly as possible. Any investments in tax-deferred accounts like

401(k)s, 403(b)s, IRAs, and the like can immediately be sold and repositioned. Any new money you add to the portfolio can be placed into the new investments as well.

However, resist the temptation to sell all the holdings in your taxable account. While it is true that the S&P 500 will likely outperform the large company stocks you currently own, it very likely may not outperform on an after-tax basis. For example, if your target is to have 30 percent of your portfolio in large U.S. stocks, your holding for that part of your portfolio is likely the S&P 500 index or a similar index. Let's say you already own large U.S. companies like Microsoft, Walmart, and Exxon Mobil, and they have very large built-in capital gains. Assuming they are not too large a part of your portfolio, it makes sense to hold them and work around them. For example, if those holdings make up $50,000, and $30,000 of that are gains, if you sell, you could lose about one-quarter or more of your gains to taxes. Instead, hold the $50,000 of positions and reduce the amount of the S&P 500 you were going to purchase by the same amount. The goal is to get as close as possible to the target portfolio without creating a tax hit that likely cannot be overcome. Yes, the S&P 500 may do better, but likely not by enough to cover the tax hit.

Another investment that may make sense to work around is an annuity. While many annuities have very high expense ratios and limited investment options, it may make sense to hold them if surrender charges are high. Wait to cash in until the surrender charges are zero or low enough to be offset by the savings in the new portfolio. If you are seriously ill, surrendering an annuity with a death benefit may not make sense at all. In short, while other investments may be better, once you have already purchased an annuity, there are many factors to take into consideration before simply selling.

There are also scenarios where I have advised clients to hold large concentrated positions that make no sense to hold from a purely target portfolio perspective. For example, a new client had $3 million of their $3.5 million net worth in one stock. They had hired my firm because the husband was dying and he wanted to be involved in choosing an advisor to assist his wife when he was gone. I advised the couple to hold the security in the husband's name until his death. On his death, the stock received a step up in basis and all the securities were able to be sold without capital gains and repositioned into a new portfolio that made much more sense for her. Investing can at times be simple, but if tax or estate planning is involved, sometimes putting together a good investment plan can do more harm than good due to the unintended consequences. Be aware of all the implications of portfolio repositioning before making changes.

Be wary of any advisor who recommends you "sell everything" regardless of tax consequences. It's irresponsible and lazy, and very poor advice. Often, with customization, the portfolio can yield a far better after-tax result.

Rule #7—Asset Location Matters

You may have noticed a common theme throughout this book: Taxes matter. They matter a lot. Advisors don't talk about it much because if you knew the tax bill they generated with all of their trading, you would fire them. The same goes for mutual funds, hedge funds, and the like. Taxes aren't noticeable by most investors because they aren't paid out of the account. For example, let's say you have an investment manager who actively trades your $1 million account. At the end of the year, you get a report saying you earned 7 percent, or $70,000. You are a pretty happy camper. A few months later, you will receive a 1099 and possibly other reports to be used for your tax preparation. If you are like most people, you will never look at it, throw it in a folder, and once all your stuff is together, you will give it to your CPA. Now, let's say that the report shows that you owe taxes of $30,000. This will be blended in with the rest of your taxes, and if your CPA asks you to cut a check to pay the IRS, you will. The $30,000 will probably not be paid out of your investment account, and even if it is, the report will forever show your rate of return was 7 percent, when in fact it was 4 percent after taxes.

Asset location can mitigate much of the damage. When building out your portfolio, resist the temptation to make every account look the same. Instead, place the investments that create substantial taxes into your tax deferred accounts. For example, put your taxable bonds and real estate investments in your IRA or 401(k). Place the investments that do not create a lot of taxes, like large company stocks, in your taxable account. By simply purchasing assets in the most tax-efficient location possible, you will improve your after-tax return.

Rule #8—Be Sure You Can Live with Your Allocation

Know thyself.

—Socrates

I have three kids—two are 8 years old and one is 13. Whenever we go to the amusement park, they examine the various rollercoasters. I can watch their minds at work. Some of the coasters are too boring for the 12-year-old and some get him excited. When he was younger, I would get a "maybe not this time" sort of look from him. Even kids attempt to make decisions as to the sort of ride they can handle.

In the past, I used to go on whatever rollercoaster they wanted. In recent years, I have often found that to be a regretful decision, particularly during the slow climb up some ridiculously high hill and the near vomit-inducing drop. Even then, though, I realize that getting off the rollercoaster and back on it in the middle of the ride is not a good idea. In fact, the odds are very good I will come out on the other end in one piece if I just follow it through to the end.

The markets are the same.

The bond market is much like the kiddie coaster at Lego Land. Almost anyone can handle it. The stock market is much like a big-time rollercoaster at Six Flags. The real estate market is like Space Mountain at Disney World: fast and in the dark. The commodity market is more like the Detonator: a ride that drops and lifts you unpredictably.

All of these rides have various levels of speed and volatility. Some find them thrilling; others find them nauseating. But in all cases, the rides generally reach a peaceful conclusion, even to the passengers who are wondering exactly what they just got themselves into.

The best time to evaluate the rollercoaster you are on is when the market is relatively stable. It is much easier to make that decision then rather than once the ride starts up again, and one day it will definitely start again.

This is easier said than done. Americans are great at forgetting things. It is a great coping mechanism that allows us to move on. After going on a rollercoaster with my son, I tell myself I won't do it again. But the next time I am at the amusement park with him, I agree to the stomach-dropping ride, not totally remembering how bad it actually felt the last time. Now, I no longer forget, and we make sure to take a friend of his along.

Smart investors customize their rollercoaster, taking parts of various markets to build a portfolio that meets their short-, intermediate-, and long-term needs. A portfolio can twist and turn, taking on the volatility necessary to meet the investor's specific goals, but should be structured within the parameters that the investor is prepared to handle.

For many, the best portfolio is a portfolio that accomplished the intended goals with the least volatility possible. However, if the volatility is outside your bandwidth of tolerance, it is far better to adjust the goal or your savings plan than to make a mistake at the worst possible time.

Rule #9—Rebalance

If you do nothing else from here, your portfolio will probably work out fine, but you will likely end up taking more risk than you intended and paying more in taxes than required. Rebalancing is a concept discussed a lot by advisors.

Here is what you likely won't hear from most advisors: Rebalancing hurts your returns over the long run! This likely will come as a surprise to you but the reason is quite simple. Over long periods of time, stocks outperform bonds. For example, if you have a portfolio that is 60 percent stocks and 40 percent bonds, and you never rebalance, you may wake up 20 years from now with a portfolio that is 85 percent stocks and 15 percent bonds. Now, there may be a scenario where it makes sense for you to have a more aggressive allocation 20 years from now than you have today, but it's unlikely. By rebalancing, you are simply keeping the portfolio aimed squarely at the target. This increases the chances that you will hit your goal. It also increases the chances that you will not substantially underperform or outperform the goal.

Some investors rebalance periodically, such as every quarter or every year. I personally think that is overkill as it can often create unnecessary transactions and sometimes taxes. If a rebalance will create taxes or extensive transactions, consider skipping it unless your allocation is totally out of whack. On the other hand, if the market drops, don't wait! Take the opportunity to rebalance at that time, intentionally increasing your exposure to the weaker asset class, usually stocks, when they are down. If they keep going down, rebalance again! This is called opportunistic rebalancing and yields a better rate of return over time than periodic rebalancing. If this is just too much to deal with, simply confirm that your goals haven't changed and rebalance one to four times a year and get on with life!

Rule #10—Revisit the Plan

You don't need a parachute to skydive. You just need one to skydive twice.
—Source unknown, author unknown

Revisit your plan and projections once a year or any time a major change in your life happens.* At your review, you will notice that your starting point may have changed. Your portfolio likely performed better or worse than expected over the previous year. You may have received an unexpected bonus, an inheritance, or had a liquidity event (for example, the sale of a property). The starting line has changed.

---

*I am always fascinated by those who want to rerun their plan monthly or quarterly. This is overkill and goes precisely against a core premise of this book, which is to have a disciplined long-term outlook, making adjustments as needed. If you are meeting with an advisor who is making changes based on a quarterly review or outlook, it's time to get a new advisor. If you are updating your own plan every week online, it is time to find a new hobby.

Perhaps your objectives are different now too. Maybe you want to retire sooner than you initially thought, or you are now going to work part time in retirement. Perhaps the college your daughter wants to go to is twice as expensive as initially thought. Maybe the baby you were going to have ended up being triplets. Maybe now you are married, or newly single, or healthier, or more ill than expected. The finish line may have moved.

All sorts of things can change that should result in changes to the portfolio. Note that the emphasis on changes to the portfolio should be based far more on personal changes than changes in various markets.

For example, let's say a 60-year-old investor has a goal of living on $100,000 per year at age 62. The projections used had assumed a portfolio rate of return of 6 percent and she was right on track for her goal. At the review, the performance shows a return far better than projected due to a strong bull market, and the portfolio yielded 20 percent. The investor is also growing weary of portfolio volatility as she approaches retirement. Luckily for her, she no longer needs a 6 percent rate of return to accomplish her goals. The projections show a 5 percent rate of return is all she needs. Given these circumstances, the investor may pull back her exposure to stocks and increase her exposure to bonds. She would be doing this knowing full well her expected long-term rate of return will be less, but the probability of getting the 5 percent will have increased, and with less volatility.

The Ultimate Rule—Don't Mess It Up!

Recently seen on CNBC:

Host: *So is this a buying opportunity?*

Guest: *I wouldn't be a buyer of this market today (S&P at 1740), but I would be a huge buyer at S&P 1725.*

This CNBC interaction illustrates precisely the wrong way to look at your portfolio. How can an allocation to stocks make no sense for an investor at S&P 1740 but a lot of sense at 1725?! Once you have the portfolio in place, *stay disciplined*. Follow the pattern of investment decisions outlined in this chapter or work with an advisor who understands, accepts, and invests with these principles. Ignore the noise, never panic, don't change plans in the middle of a crisis, and stay focused on your goals.

Portfolio Examples

Common sense attests that some people can and do beat the market. It's not all chance. Many academics agree; but the method of beating the market, they say, is not to exercise superior clairvoyance but rather to assume greater risk. Risk, and risk alone, determines the degree to which returns will be above or below average.
— Burton G. Malkiel, *A Random Walk Down Wall Street*

The "I Want to Beat the Market" Portfolio

This book explains why you can't beat the market by market timing or actively trading stocks. If you want to beat the market, and you define the market as the S&P 500, then the way to attempt to beat it over time is to increase exposure of the portfolio to holdings that are likely to outperform large-cap U.S. stocks over long periods of time. Examples of asset classes that are riskier than U.S. stocks that have a good probability of outperforming are small U.S. stocks and emerging markets stocks. A "beat the market" portfolio may look like the one shown in Figure 6.4.

The "I Need 7 Percent to Hit My Long-Term Retirement Goal" Portfolio

A portfolio diversified across various asset classes and with a global approach has a solid probability of achieving the returns the typical investor requires. Such a portfolio may look like the one shown in Figure 6.5.

The "Get Me What I Need for the Rest of My Life with the Least Volatility Possible" Portfolio

This portfolio should have enough stocks to pull the rate of return to where it needs to be over a long period of time, but enough bonds to

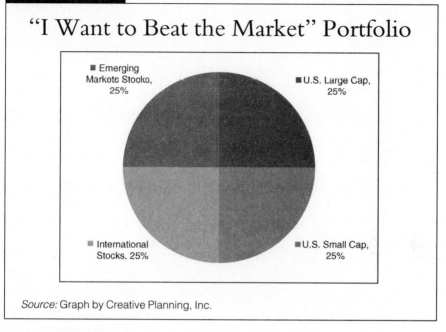

FIGURE 6.4

"I Want to Beat the Market" Portfolio

- Emerging Markets Stocks, 25%
- U.S. Large Cap, 25%
- International Stocks, 25%
- U.S. Small Cap, 25%

Source: Graph by Creative Planning, Inc.

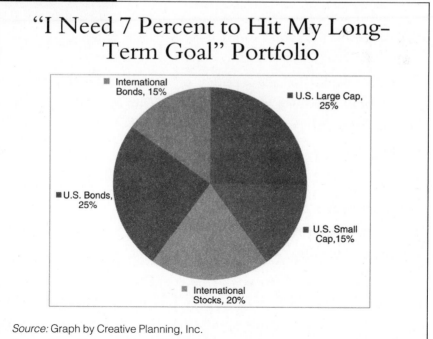

FIGURE 6.5

"I Need 7 Percent to Hit My Long-Term Goal" Portfolio

- International Bonds, 15%
- U.S. Large Cap, 25%
- U.S. Bonds, 25%
- U.S. Small Cap, 15%
- International Stocks, 20%

Source: Graph by Creative Planning, Inc.

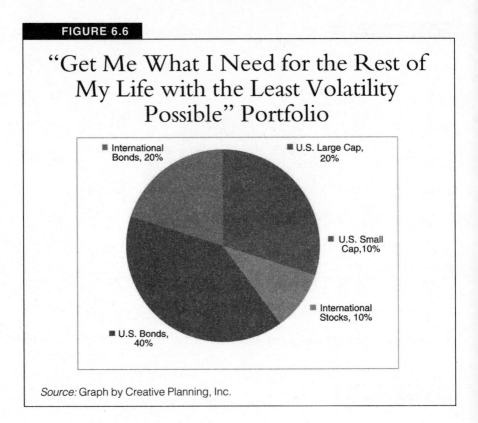

| FIGURE 6.6 |

"Get Me What I Need for the Rest of My Life with the Least Volatility Possible" Portfolio

International Bonds, 20%
U.S. Large Cap, 20%
U.S. Small Cap, 10%
International Stocks, 10%
U.S. Bonds, 40%

Source: Graph by Creative Planning, Inc.

allow the investor to take monthly or annual distributions without selling stocks in a down market. For an investor with $1,000,000 and who needs $50,000 per year, the portfolio may look like the one shown in Figure 6.6.

The "I Have More Money Than I Will Ever Need and I Want It to Grow with Minimal Volatility" Portfolio

This portfolio is for someone who has enough money that the income alone from stocks and bonds will meet their needs for life, even when adjusted for inflation. Despite reading this book, this person is fearful of

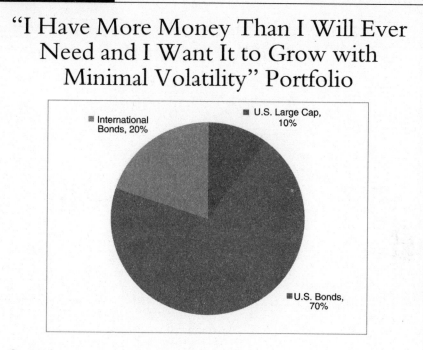

"I Have More Money Than I Will Ever Need and I Want It to Grow with Minimal Volatility" Portfolio

International Bonds, 20%

U.S. Large Cap, 10%

U.S. Bonds, 70%

Source: Graph by Creative Planning, Inc.

stocks and wants a low volatility portfolio that will allow her to draw about 3 percent without invading principal (see Figure 6.7).

The "I Have More Money Than I Will Ever Need, Volatility Doesn't Bother Me, and I Want It to Grow Along with the Market" Portfolio

Some people are fortunate enough to have more investable assets than they could ever possibly spend. A subset of this group is not bothered by volatility, accepts that stocks will likely outperform bonds, and wants to participate in the market return, all without taking significant excess risk to try to beat the market return. For this group, a portfolio might look like the one shown in Figure 6.8.

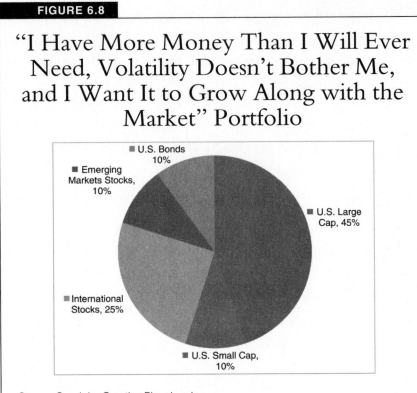

FIGURE 6.8

"I Have More Money Than I Will Ever Need, Volatility Doesn't Bother Me, and I Want It to Grow Along with the Market" Portfolio

Source: Graph by Creative Planning, Inc.

A Path to Success—Intelligent Portfolio Construction

Some of the principles of portfolio construction are very straightforward:

- Avoid market timing; instead, invest for the long run.
- Avoid active trading; buy mostly passive investments.
- Don't fall for performance claims, get scared by the media, and the like; tune out the noise.
- Don't get in your own way; be aware of your behavioral biases, recognize them when they appear, and control them.
- Build a portfolio with asset classes that make sense for your situation.

For some, especially higher-net-worth investors, the portfolio construction can get more sophisticated. To match yourself to a portfolio that
will not only accomplish your goals but that you can also live with, it is
important to measure the return you need against the volatility you can
handle. For good measure, make sure you take taxes into consideration,
as well as changing circumstances. While the portfolio itself should not be
highly active, you must put more into it than simply choosing a few
indexes and leaving it at that!

The Ultimate Mistake

Life is what happens while you are busy making other plans.

—John Lennon

In 1970, a prominent politician offered my dad, his physician, some free advice. "Alex," he said, "I have all the money in the world, but I never enjoyed it. Make time to enjoy yourself." My dad took the advice to heart and expanded his vacation schedule.

I have observed the wisdom in this advice throughout my career. While I lead an investment committee, I am also a Certified Financial Planner® and an estate planning attorney. My firm regularly works with clients throughout their lives, through incapacity, and with their families on death.

Many of these very successful people have done a great job of saving a good amount of wealth and of somehow never messing things up along the way. These are two very difficult things to achieve. I have seen that these people certainly don't deprive themselves, but they are not really enjoying their position to their fullest. Many of these folks got where they are by being thrifty and diligent. It is not uncommon for a client to save in their IRA every year for their entire life. Then, when they turn $70\frac{1}{2}$ and the government forces a withdrawal, they ask me how to avoid taking the money out. They have been putting money in for so long, they can't bear the thought of spending it!

Let me tell you something about your money.

Know that it makes no difference whether your heirs inherit $250,000 instead of $300,000, $600,000 instead of $800,000, $1.2 million instead $1.4 million, or $10 million instead of $11 million, so enjoy yourself and the wealth you have spent your life creating and preserving.

After preparing a net worth statement with a client, he said to me, "I would like to die and come back as my kids." Your estate on death isn't just your investment account. It is also the value of your home, insurance, cars, and so on. All will likely be liquidated, thrown into a pot, and split up.

If you are financially independent, let me contradict just about everything you hear from financial advisors when I tell you to get that extra-tall cup of expensive coffee, quit driving that 10-year-old car,* and upgrade your next vacation.

Believe me when I tell you that your kids will! I have seen kids buy new cars and homes within days of receiving an inheritance.

If you are charitably inclined and financially independent, go ahead and experience the pleasure of giving now. *Enjoy it!* Why wait until you are dead? If you insist on passing your wealth to your kids at your own expense, go ahead and do it now. Enjoy passing the wealth onto your kids and grandkids rather than them receiving larger checks when you are no longer around.

---

* Seriously, get a new car! You know, one with current technology and safety features! If it's 10 years old, you aren't even protecting yourself. This is your life we are talking about here! You don't use a 10-year-old computer, do you? Oh my goodness! If you do, get a new computer too! Geez!!

The bottom line is this: *It's your money*. You busted your butt for it, you saved it, and you preserved it. So long as you are not jeopardizing your financial security, enjoy yourself a bit, give away what you want too, and overall, loosen up a bit and experience the fruits of your labor.

Let's Roll!

Simple can be harder than complex. You have to work hard to get your thinking clean to make it simple.

—Steve Jobs

Market timing, active trading, acting on bad information, making behavioral mistakes, or hiring the wrong advisor can all lead to permanent damage to your financial well-being. Being aware of these key pitfalls is the best way to recognize and avoid them. You can do better than that though!

By following the guidelines on how best to manage your wealth, you can not only avoid the mistakes, but optimize your wealth. If an advisor is the best fit for you, demand one who follows these principles, and you can enjoy life knowing you are following a path to success.

Reading this is one thing; acting on it is another. Financial advisors and financial media are actively working to suck you back into methods that sound good but don't work. Resist the temptation to fall prey to their temptations. You have the knowledge to do this. Don't let anyone tell you that the system isn't complicated enough or sexy enough. That's a bunch of hooey. With investing, the less clutter the better.

With discipline, you and your advisor can follow this system through all kinds of markets, and most importantly, stick with it through down markets. You will be financially and emotionally better off for it!

Keep in mind, it is not enough to follow the system some of the time. If you eat a donut for breakfast, cake for lunch, and ice cream for dinner, nothing will happen. If you do it every day for a few years, you will be dead. If you text and drive once, it might turn out just fine. If you do it all the time, eventually you are likely to crash. The key to successful investing is to focus on repeatable behavior using a disciplined, ongoing system. Take what you have learned, develop a plan of action, and stick to the plan. You can do this. Let's roll!*

The best time to plant a tree was yesterday. The second best time is today.

—*Chinese Proverb*[†]

---

* I mean like right now! Let's roll! Quit putting it off. Get a plan together and get on the right track today!

† While Americans say macho things like, "Let's roll," the Chinese came up with a much more eloquent way to say the same thing!

References

AboutInflation.com. 2013. "Gold vs. Inflation." Retrieved from www.aboutinflation.com/gold-vs-inflation.

Alpert, Bill. 2007. "Shorting Cramer." *Barron's*, August 20.

Alpert, Bill. 2009. "Cramer's Star Outshines His Stock Picks." *Barron's*, February 9.

Alpert, Marc, and Howard Raiffa. 1982. "A Progress Report on the Training of Probability Assessors." In *Judgment Under Uncertainty: Heuristics and Biases*, edited by Daniel Kahneman, Paul Slovic, and Amos Tversky, 294–305. Cambridge: Cambridge University Press.

Amabile, Teresa M., and Steven J. Kramer. 2011. "The Power of Small Wins." *Harvard Business Review* 89 (5): 70–80.

Arkes, Hal R., Cynthia A. Joyner, Mark V. Pezzo, Jane Gradwohl Nash, Karen Siegel-Jacobs, and Eric Stone. 1994. "The Psychology of Windfall Gains." *Organizational Behavior and Human Decision Processes* 59:331–347.

Armor, David A., and Shelley E. Taylor. 2002. "When Predictions Fail: The Dilemma of Unrealistic Optimism." In *Heuristics and Biases: The Psychology of Intuitive Judgment*, edited by Thomas Gilovich, Dale Griffin, and Daniel Kahneman, 334–348. Cambridge: Cambridge University Press.

Arnold, Tom, John H. Earl, and David S. North. 2007. "Are Cover Stories Effective Contrarian Indicators?" *Financial Analysts Journal* 63 (2): 70–75.

Averill, James R. 1980. "A Constructivist View of Emotion." In *Emotion: Theory, Research and Experience 1*, edited by R. Plutchik and H. Kellerman, 305–339. New York: Academic Press.

Barber, Brad M., and Terrance Odean. 2001. "Boys Will Be Boys: Gender, Overconfidence, and Common Stock Investment." *The Quarterly Journal of Economics* 116 (1, February): 261–292.

Barrett, Amy L., and Brent R. Brodeski. 2006. "Survivor Bias and Improper Measurements: How the Mutual Fund Industry Inflates Actively Managed Fund Performance." Zero Alpha Group and Savant Capital Management, Inc. Retrieved from www.etf.com/docs/sbiasstudy.pdf?iu=1.

Bauer, Richard J., and Julie R. Dahlquist. 2001. "Market Timing and Roulette Wheels." *Financial Analysts Journal* 57 (1, January–February): 28–40.

Bespoke Investment Group. 2012. "Wall Street Strategists Remain Bearish." Retrieved from www.bespokeinvest.com/thinkbig/2012/3/12/wall-street -strategists-remain-bearish.html.

Britton, Diana. 2011. "Is Tactical Investing Wall Street's Next Clown Act?" WealthManagement.com. Retrieved from http://wealthmanagement .com/investment/tactical-investing-wall-streets-next-clown-act.

Chen, Peng. 2013. "Are You Getting Your Money's Worth? Sources of Hedge Fund Returns." Austin, TX: Dimensional Fund Advisors LP.

Christensen-Szalanski, Jay J., and James B. Bushyhead. 1981. "Physicians' Use of Probabilistic Information in a Real Clinical Setting." *Journal of Experimental Psychology: Human Perception and Performance* 7 (4, August): 928–935.

Cieszynski, Colin. 2012. "What Does the US Presidential Election Mean for Markets?" *CMC Markets*. Retrieved from http://blog.cmcmarkets.com.au/ asset-class/companies/what-does-the-us-presidential-election-mean-for -markets/.

Cowles, A. 3rd. 1933. "Can Stock Market Forecasters Forecast?" *Econometrics* 1 (2, April): 309–324.

Crary, David. 2008. "Students Lie, Cheat, Steal, But Say They're Good." Associated Press, November 30.

Cross, K. Patricia. 1977. "Not Can, But *Will* College Teaching Be Improved?" *New Directions for Higher Education* 17:1–15.

CXO Advisory Group, LLC. 2013. "'Sell in May' Over the Long Run." Retrieved from www.cxoadvisory.com/3873/calendar-effects/sell-in -may-over-the-long-run/.

Daniel, Kent, David Hirshleifer, and Avanidhar Subrahmanyam. 1998. "Investor Psychology and Security Market Under- and Overreactions." *Journal of Finance* 53 (6): 1839–1885.

Denrell, Jerker, and Christina Fang. 2010. "Predicting the Next Big Thing: Success as a Signal of Poor Judgment." *Management Science* 56 (10): 1653–1667.

Dent, Harry S. Jr. 2006. *The Next Great Bubble Boom: How to Profit from the Greatest Boom in History: 2006–2010*. New York: Free Press.

Dent, Harry S. Jr. 2008. *The Great Depression Ahead: How to Prosper in the Crash Following the Greatest Boom in History*. New York: Free Press.

Dent, Harry. 2013. "Survive and Prosper." Retrieved from http://survive -prosper.com/pages/latest-research/landing/google/N704-PPC-Winter -Dow-Today-3300-CN.php?code=X195N704.

Ellis, Charles D. 2012. "Murder on the Orient Express: The Mystery of Underperformance." *Financial Analysts Journal* 68 (4, July–August): 13–19.

Ferri, Rick. 2013. "Busting the Sell in May and Go Away Myth." *Forbes*, April 8. Retrieved from www.forbes.com/sites/rickferri/2013/04/08/busting-the -sell-in-may-and-go-away-myth/.

Fidelity Viewpoints. 2013. "Get Ready for the Next Market Crisis." Fidelity Investments. Retrieved from https://www.fidelity.com/viewpoints/ investing-ideas/get-ready-for-the-next-crisis.

Fisher Asset Management, LLC. "Fisher Investments Philosophy." Retrieved from www.fisherinvestments.com/investing/philosophy/.

Fisher, Ken. 2007. "The Fall 2007 Rally." *Forbes*, September 17. Retrieved from www.forbes.com/free_forbes/2007/0917/210.html.

Fisher, Ken. 2008. "We're Too Gloomy." *Forbes*, January 28.

Fox, Justin. 2014. "What Alan Greenspan Has Learned Since 2008." *The Harvard Business Review Blog Network*. Retrieved from http://blogs.hbr.org/2014/ 01/what-alan-greenspan-has-learned-since-2008/.

Franklin Templeton Investments. 2014. "Time to Take Stock." Retrieved from https://www.franklintempleton.com/forms-literature/download/TS-B.

Grable, John E., and Sonya L. Britt. 2012. "Financial News and Client Stress: Understanding the Association from a Financial Planning Perspective." Kansas State University Financial Planning Research Center.

Graham, John R., and Campbell R. Harvey. 1994. "Market Timing Ability and Volatility Implied in Investment Newsletters' Asset Allocation Recommendations." Fuqua School of Business, Duke University.

Haizlip, Julie, Natalie May, John Schorling, Anne Williams, and Margaret Plews-Ogan. 2012. "Perspective: The Negativity Bias, Medical Education, and the Culture of Academic Medicine: Why Culture Change Is Hard." *Academic Medicine* 87 (9, September): 1205–1209.

Hamlin, J. Kiley, Karen Wynn, and Paul Bloom. 2010. "Three-Month-Olds Show a Negativity Bias in Their Social Evaluations." *Developmental Science* 13 (6): 923–929.

Hartung, Adam. 2012. "Want a Better Economy? History Says Vote Democrat!" *Forbes*, October 10. Retrieved from www.forbes.com/sites/adamhartung/2012/10/10/want-a-better-economy-history-says-vote-democrat/.

Heuer, Richard J. Jr. 1999. *Psychology of Intelligence Analysis*. Washington, DC: Center for the Study of Intelligence, Central Intelligence Agency.

Housel, Morgan. 2014. "The World's Smartest Investors Have Failed." *The Motley Fool*. Retrieved from www.fool.com/investing/general/2014/01/27/the-worlds-smartest-investors-have-failed.aspx.

Israelsen, Craig L. 2010. "What's in a Name?" *Financial Planning*, June 1.

Jeffrey, Robert H. 1984. "The Folly of Stock Market Timing." *Harvard Business Review* (July–August): 102–110.

Kahneman, Daniel, and Amos Tversky. 1984. "Choices, Values, and Frames." *The American Psychologist* 39 (4): 341–350.

Kahneman, Daniel, and Dan Lovallo. 1993. "Timid Choices and Bold Forecasts: A Cognitive Perspective on Risk Taking." *Management Science* 39 (1): 17–31.

Kahneman, Daniel, Jack L. Knetsch, and Richard H. Thaler. 1991. "Anomalies: The Endowment Effect, Loss Aversion, and Status Quo Bias." *Journal of Economic Perspectives* 5 (1): 193–206.

Kinniry, Francis M. Jr., Colleen M. Jaconetti, Michael A. DiJoseph, and Yan Zilbering. 2014. "Putting a Value on Your Value: Quantifying Vanguard Advisor's Alpha." The Vanguard Group, Inc. Retrieved from https://advisors.vanguard.com/iwe/pdf/ISGQVAA.pdf?cbdForceDomain=true.

Kopecki, Dawn, Clea Benson, and Phil Mattingly. 2012. "Dimon Says Over-confidence Fueled Loss He Can't Defend." *Bloomberg*. Retrieved from www.bloomberg.com/news/2012-06-14/dimon-says-overconfidence-fueled-loss-he-can-t-defend.html.

Krantz, Matt. 2013. "Investors Face a Shrinking Stock Supply." *USA Today*, March 17. Retrieved from www.usatoday.com/story/money/personalfinance/2013/03/17/public-companies-vanishing-fewer-stocks/1920681/.

Lauricella, Tom. 2005. "Yale Manager Blasts Industry; His Advice to Individuals: Choose Index Funds, ETFs Over Active Managers." *Wall Street Journal*

Online. Retrieved from http://online.wsj.com/news/articles/SB112597 100191832366.

Marano, Hara Estroff. 2004. "Marriage Math." Psychology Today, March 16. Retrieved from www.psychologytoday.com/articles/200403/marriage -math.

Marquet, Christopher T. 2011. "The Marquet Report on Ponzi Schemes." Marquet International, Ltd. Retrieved from www.marquetinternational. com/pdf/marquet_report_on_ponzi_schemes.pdf.

McCall, Tommy. 2008. "Bulls, Bears, Donkeys and Elephants." *New York Times*, October 14. Retrieved from www.nytimes.com/interactive/2008/ 10/14/opinion/20081014_OPCHART.html?_r=0.

McElroy, Todd, and Keith Dowd. 2007. "Susceptibility to Anchoring Effects: How Openness-to-Experience Influences Responses to Anchoring Cues." *Judgment and Decision Making* 2 (1, February): 48–53.

Montier, James. 2006. *Behaving Badly*. London: Dresdner Kleinwort Wasserstein Securities.

Mulcahy, Diane, Bill Weeks, and Harold S. Bradley. 2012. "We Have Met the Enemy . . . and He Is Us: Lessons from Twenty Years of the Kauffman Foundation's Investments in Venture Capital Funds and the Triumph of Hope Over Experience." Ewing Marion Kauffman Foundation. Retrieved from www.kauffman.org/~/media/kauffman_org/research%20reports% 20and%20covers/2012/05/we%20have%20met%20the%20enemy%20and %20he%20is%20us(1).pdf.

The National Association of Personal Financial Planners. *Pursuit of a Financial Advisor: Field Guide*. Arlington Heights, IL: National Association of Personal Financial Planners. Retrieved from www.napfa.org/UserFiles/File/ FinancialAdvisorFieldGuidev13.pdf.

Nouriel Roubini Predictions. Wall Street Economists Institute. Retrieved from http://economicpredictions.org/nouriel-roubini-predictions/index.htm.

NYT Roubini Article, IMF Transcript. Economic Cycle Research Institute. Retrieved from https://www.businesscycle.com/ecri-news-events/news -details/nyt-roubini-article-imf-transcript.

Odean, Terrance. 1998. "Volume, Volatility, Price, and Profit When All Traders Are Above Average." *Journal of Finance* 53 (6): 1887–1934.

O'Keefe, Brian. 2008. "Is Buy-and-Hold Dead and Gone?" *Fortune*, October 28.

Park, Jae Hong, Prabhudev Konana, Bin Gu, Alok Kumar, and Rajagopal Raghunathan. 2010. "Confirmation Bias, Overconfidence, and Investment Performance: Evidence from Stock Message Boards." McCombs Research Paper Series No. IROM-07-10. Retrieved from http://ssrn.com/abstract=1639470.

Patel, Sital S. 2013. "Madoff: Don't Let Wall Street Scam You, Like I Did." *MarketWatch*. Retrieved from www.marketwatch.com/story/madoff-dont-let-wall-street-scam-you-like-i-did-2013-06-05?pagenumber=2.

PBS's *Frontline*. 2013. "The Retirement Gamble." [JW Player video file.] Retrieved from www.pbs.org/wgbh/pages/frontline/retirement-gamble/.

Peter Schiff Predictions. Wall Street Economists Institute. Retrieved from http://economicpredictions.org/peter-schiff-predictions/index.htm.

Philips, Christopher B., Francis M. Kinniry, Jr., and Todd Schlanger. 2013. "The Case for Index-Fund Investing." The Vanguard Group, Inc. Retrieved from https://personal.vanguard.com/pdf/s296.pdf.

Plous, Scott. 1993. *The Psychology of Judgment and Decision Making*. New York: McGraw-Hill.

Ptak, Jeffrey. 2012. "In Practice: Tactical Funds Miss Their Chance." *Morningstar Advisor*. Retrieved from http://advisors.morningstar.com/advisor/t/51504278/in-practice-tactical-funds-miss-their-chance.htm?&q=tactical&single=true.

Riepe, Mark W. 2013. "Does Market Timing Work?" Charles Schwab. Retrieved from www.schwab.com/public/schwab/nn/articles/Does-Market-Timing-Work.

Roth, Allan. 2012. "Second Dent Investment Fund to Disappear." *CBS Money Watch*. Retrieved from www.cbsnews.com/news/second-dent-investment-fund-to-disappear/.

Schlanger, Todd, and Christopher B. Philips. 2013. "The Mutual Fund Graveyard: An Analysis of Dead Funds." The Vanguard Group, Inc. Retrieved from https://personal.vanguard.com/pdf/s362.pdf.

Serwer, Andy. 2006. "The Greatest Money Manager of Our Time." *Fortune*, November 28.

Sharpe, William F. 1975. "Likely Gains from Market Timing." *Financial Analysts Journal* 31 (2): 60–69.

Shtekhman, Anatoly, Christos Tasopoulos, and Brian Wimmer. 2012. "Dollar-Cost Averaging Just Means Taking Risk Later." The Vanguard Group, Inc.

Retrieved from https://institutional.vanguard.com/iam/pdf/ICRDCA .pdf?cbdForceDomain=true.

Slovic, Paul. 1973. "Behavioral Problems of Adhering to a Decision Policy." Paper presented at the Institute for Quantitative Research in Finance, May 1, Napa, California.

Snider, Kim. 2014. "The Great Market Timing Lie." Snider Advisors. Retrieved from https://www.snideradvisors.com/KimSnider/Web/FreeStuff/Market Timing.aspx.

S&P Dow Jones Indices, LLC. 2014. "S&P Dow Jones Indices." McGraw Hill Financial. Retrieved from www.djindexes.com/.

Sullivan, Todd. 2008. "Being Wrong for Five Years Makes Peter Schiff Right Now?" Seeking Alpha. Retrieved from http://seekingalpha.com/article/ 106824-being-wrong-for-five-years-makes-peter-schiff-right-now.

Sumner, Mark. 2008. "Whither Goest Thou, Stock Market?" Kos Media, LLC. Retrieved from www.dailykos.com/story/2008/12/02/668445/-Whither -Goest-Thou-Stock-Market#.

Svenson, Ola. 1981. "Are We All Less Risky and More Skillful Than Our Fellow Drivers?" *Acta Psychologica* 47 (2): 143–148.

Taleb, Nassim Nicholas. 2007. *The Black Swan*. New York: Random House.

Tottenham, Nim, Jessica Phuong, Jessica Flannery, Laurel Gabard-Durnam, and Bonnie Goff. 2013. "A Negativity Bias for Ambiguous Facial-Expression Valence during Childhood: Converging Evidence from Behavior and Facial Corrugator Muscle Responses." *Emotion* 13 (1): 92–103.

Van Eaton, R. Douglas. 2000. "The Psychology Behind Common Investor Mistakes." *American Association of Individual Investors Journal* 22 (April): 2–5.

The Vanguard Group, Inc. 2013a. "Tax Efficiency: A Decisive Advantage for Index Funds." Retrieved from https://advisors.vanguard.com/VGApp/ iip/site/advisor/researchcommentary/article/IWE_InvComTaxEfficiency.

The Vanguard Group, Inc. 2013b. "Vanguard's Principles for Investing Success." Retrieved from https://personal.vanguard.com/pdf/s700.pdf.

Vardi, Nathan. 2012. "Billionaire John Paulson's Hedge Fund: Too Big to Manage." *Forbes*, December 21.

Voigt, Kevin. 2011. "October: The Scariest Month for Stocks?" CNN. Retrieved from http://business.blogs.cnn.com/2011/10/04/october-the -scariest-month-for-stocks/.

Wagenaar, Willem, and Gideon B. Keren. 1986. "Does the Expert Know? The Reliability of Predictions and Confidence Ratings of Experts." In *Intelligent Decision Support in Process Environments*, edited by Erik Hollnagel, Giuseppe Mancini, and David D. Woods, 87–103. Berlin: Springer.

Waggoner, John. 2005. "Top-Selling Funds of 2000 in Deep Red." *USA Today*, April 5.

Wallick, Daniel W., Brian R. Wimmer, and Todd Schlanger. 2012. "Assessing Endowment Performance: The Enduring Role of Low-Cost Investing." The Vanguard Group, Inc. Retrieved from https://institutional.vanguard .com/iam/pdf/ICR25P.pdf?cbdForceDomain=true.

Wansink, Brian, Robert J. Kent, and Stephen J. Hoch. 1998. "An Anchoring and Adjustment Model of Purchase Quantity Decisions." *Journal of Marketing Research* 35 (February): 71–81.

Weber, Tim. 2011. "Davos 2011: Why Do Economists Get It So Wrong?" BBC. Retrieved from www.bbc.co.uk/news/business-12294332.

Willoughby, Jack. 2010. "Lifting Beyond Their Weight Class." *Barron's*, July 10.

Wimmer, Brian R., Sandeep S. Chhabra, and Daniel W. Wallick. 2013. "The Bumpy Road to Outperformance." The Vanguard Group, Inc. Retrieved from https://institutional.vanguard.com/iam/pdf/outperformance_research_ paper.pdf?cbdForceDomain=true.

Young, David. 2007. "To Succeed, Keep It Simple." *Investment Advisor*, February 1.

Zacharakis, Andrew, and Dean Shepherd. 2001. "The Nature of Information and Overconfidence on Venture Capitalists' Decision Making." *Journal of Business Venturing*, 16 (4): 311–332.

Zelizer, Viviana A. 1994. *The Social Meaning of Money: Pin Money, Paychecks, Poor Relief, and Other Currencies*. New York: Basic Books.

Index